THE GIRONDINS OF CHILE

THE GIRONDINS
OF CHILE

REMINISCENCES OF AN EYEWITNESS

BENJAMÍN VICUÑA MACKENNA

Translated from the Spanish by
JOHN H. R. POLT

EDITED WITH AN INTRODUCTION AND NOTES
BY CRISTIÁN GAZMURI

OXFORD
UNIVERSITY PRESS

2003

OXFORD
UNIVERSITY PRESS

Oxford New York
Auckland Bangkok Buenos Aires Cape Town Chennai
Dar es Salaam Delhi Hong Kong Istanbul Karachi Kolkata
Kuala Lumpur Madrid Melbourne Mexico City Mumbai Nairobi
São Paulo Shanghai Taipei Tokyo Toronto

Copyright © 2003 by Oxford University Press, Inc.

Published by Oxford University Press, Inc.
198 Madison Avenue, New York, New York 10016

www.oup.com

Oxford is a registered trademark of Oxford University Press

Library of Congress Cataloging-in-Publication Data
Vicuña Mackenna, Benjamin, 1831–1886
[Jirondinos chilenos. English]
The Girondins of Chile : reminiscences of an eyewitness /
Benjamin Vicuña Mackenna; translated from the Spanish by John H. R. Polt;
with an introduction and notes by Cristián Gazmuri.
New York : Oxford University Press, 2002
p.   cm.   (Library of Latin America)
ISBN 0-19-515180-1 ISBN: 978-0-19-515181-7
Includes bibliographical references.
1. Chile—Politics and government—1824–1920. 2. Chile—History—Insurrection, 1851.
3. France—History—February Revolution, 1848—Influence.
4. Gazmuri R., Cristián (Gazmuri Riveros)
F 3095.v6513   2002   983/.04 21

Printed in the United States of America
on acid-free paper

Contents

Series Editors'
General Introduction

The Library of Latin America series makes available in translation major nineteenth-century authors whose work has been neglected in the English-speaking world. The titles for the translations from the Spanish and Portuguese were suggested by an editorial committee that included Jean Franco (general editor responsible for works in Spanish), Richard Graham (series editor responsible for works in Portuguese), Tulio Halperín Donghi (at the University of California, Berkeley), Iván Jaksić (at the University of Notre Dame), Naomi Lindstrom (at the University of Texas at Austin), Eduardo Lozano of the Library at the University of Pittsburgh, and Francine Masiello (at the University of California, Berkeley). The late Antonio Cornejo Polar of the University of California, Berkeley, was also one of the founding members of the committee. The translations have been funded thanks to the generosity of the Lampadia Foundation and the Andrew W. Mellon Foundation.

During the period of national formation between 1810 and into the early years of the twentieth century, the new nations of Latin America fashioned their identities, drew up constitutions, engaged in bitter struggles over territory, and debated questions of education, government, ethnicity, and culture. This was a unique period unlike the process of nation formation in Europe and one that should be more familiar than it is to students of comparative politics, history, and literature.

The image of the nation was envisioned by the lettered classes—a minority in countries in which indigenous, mestizo, black, or mulatto peasants and slaves predominated—although there were also alternative nationalisms at the grassroots level. The cultural elite were well educated in European thought and letters, but as statesmen, journalists, poets, and academics, they confronted the problem of the racial and linguistic heterogeneity of the continent and the difficulties of integrating the population into a modern nation-state. Some of the writers whose works will be translated in the Library of Latin America series played leading roles in politics. Fray Servando Teresa de Mier, a friar who translated Rousseau's *The Social Contract* and was one of the most colorful characters of the independence period, was faced with imprisonment and expulsion from Mexico for his heterodox beliefs; on his return, after independence, he was elected to the congress. Domingo Faustino Sarmiento, exiled from his native Argentina under the dictatorship of

Rosas, wrote *Facundo: Civilización y barbarie,* a stinging denunciation of that government. He returned after Rosas' overthrow and was elected president in 1868. Andrés Bello was born in Venezuela, lived in London, where he published poetry during the independence period, settled in Chile, where he founded the University, wrote his grammar of the Spanish language, and drew up the country's legal code.

These post-independence intellectuals were not simply dreaming castles in the air, but vitally contributed to the founding of nations and the shaping of culture. The advantage of hindsight may make us aware of problems they themselves did not foresee, but this should not affect our assessment of their truly astonishing energies and achievements. Although there is a recent translation of Sarmiento's celebrated *Facundo,* there is no translation of his memoirs, *Recuerdos de provincia (Provincial Recollections).* The predominance of memoirs in the Library of Latin America series is no accident—many of these offer entertaining insights into a vast and complex continent.

Nor have we neglected the novel. The series includes new translations of the outstanding Brazilian writer Joaquim Maria Machado de Assis' work, including *Dom Casmurro* and *The Posthumous Memoirs of Brás Cubas.* There is no reason why other novels and writers who are not so well known outside Latin America—the Peruvian novelist Clorinda Matto de Turner's *Aves sin nido,* Nataniel Aguirre's *Juan de la Rosa,* José de Alencar's *Iracema,* Juana Manuela Gorriti's short stories—should not be read with as much interest as the political novels of Anthony Trollope.

A series on nineteenth-century Latin America cannot, however, be limited to literary genres such as the novel, the poem, and the short story. The literature of independent Latin America was eclectic and strongly influenced by the periodical press newly liberated from scrutiny by colonial authorities and the Inquisition. Newspapers were miscellanies of fiction, essays, poems, and translations from all manner of European writing. The novels written on the eve of Mexican Independence by José Joaquín Fernández de Lizardi included disquisitions on secular education and law and denunciations of the evils of gaming and idleness. Other works, such as a well-known poem by Andrés Bello, "Ode to Tropical Agriculture," and novels such as *Amalia* by José Mármol and the Bolivian Nataniel Aguirre's *Juan de la Rosa*, were openly partisan. By the end of the century, sophisticated scholars were beginning to address the history of their countries, as did João Capistrano de Abreu in his *Capítulos de história colonial.*

It is often in memoirs such as those by Fray Servando Teresa de Mier or Sarmiento that we find the descriptions of everyday life that in Europe were incorporated into the realist novel. Latin American literature at this time was seen largely as a pedagogical tool, a "light" alternative to speeches, sermons, and philosophical tracts—though, in fact, especially in the early part of the century, even the readership for novels was quite small because of the high rate of illiteracy. Nevertheless, the vigorous orally transmitted culture of the gaucho and the urban underclasses became the linguistic repertoire of some of the most interesting nineteenth-century writers—most notably José Hernández, author of the "gauchesque" poem "Martín Fierro," which enjoyed an unparalleled popularity. But for many writers the task was not to appropriate popular language but to civilize, and their literary works were strongly influenced by the high style of political oratory.

The editorial committee has not attempted to limit its selection to the better-known writers such as Machado de Assis; it has also selected many works that have never appeared in translation or writers whose work has not been translated recently. The series now makes these works available to the English-speaking public.

Because of the preferences of funding organizations, the series initially focuses on writing from Brazil, the Southern Cone, the Andean region, and Mexico. Each of our editions will have an introduction that places the work in its appropriate context and includes explanatory notes.

We owe special thanks to the late Robert Glynn of the Lampadia Foundation, whose initiative gave the project a jump start, and to Richard Ekman of the Andrew W. Mellon Foundation, which also generously supported the project. We also thank the Rockefeller Foundation for funding the 1996 symposium "Culture and Nation in Iberoamerica," organized by the editorial board of the Library of Latin America. We received substantial institutional support and personal encouragement from the Institute of Latin American Studies of the University of Texas at Austin. The support of Edward Barry of Oxford University Press has been crucial, as has the advice and help of Ellen Chodosh of Oxford University

Press. The first volumes of the series were published after the untimely death, on July 3, 1997, of Maria C. Bulle, who, as an associate of the Lampadia Foundation, supported the idea from its beginning.

—Jean Franco
—Richard Graham

The Chilean Girondins
and Their Time

B enjamín Vicuña Mackenna stated at the beginning of *Los Girondinos chilenos* that the 1848 revolutions (the so-called '48) in Europe had a tremendous impact in Chile.[1] In this introduction, I will assess the magnitude of this impact, refer to the arrival of Alphonse de Lamartine's *Histoire des Girondins* in the country and its influence there, and provide a brief history of the political actions of the group of young liberals whom Vicuña Mackenna called the "Chilean Girondins."

When the news of the fall of Louis-Philippe d'Orléans and the installation of the Second Republic became known in Chile, there was jubilation in Santiago. In May 1848, Léonce Levraud, the consul general of France in Chile, informed the Quai d'Orsay of the enormous enthusiasm he had witnessed in Santiago. "This afternoon at the theater," he remarked, "the Italian company and the spectators sang the national anthem and the Marseillaise." He did not fail to observe, however, that at least some aristocrats "appear to be terrified." There was the fear, he added, of a connection between "the principles of the French Republic and the proclaimed liberties of Chile, which are little more than a lie and a joke."[2] There is, however, limited evidence of such fear in either the conservative press or in the government. This would only appear some weeks later. The immediate response was one of widespread support. Andrés Bello, who could hardly be considered a revolutionary, visited Levraud to congratulate him for the good news.

Republican Chile congratulated itself on the installation of a republic in France. The press provided abundant examples of praise: *El Mercurio* stated on May 30, 1848, that "to oppose the [revolutionary] torrent would be suicidal. There are no barriers to ideas, much less to the generous ideas proclaimed by the sincere people of France." On June 4, the paper added that "the French revolution of 1848 was made for the good of humanity; led by enlightened ideas and sanctioned by religion, it will bring true liberty to Chile despite whatever efforts are made to contain it. The seeds of that spirit and sentiment have been planted for some time, and today they see the light with vigor and freshness. Nothing can stop it." And on June 9, the newspaper echoed the enthusiastic opinion of many (though not Levraud's) when it stated that "the French revolution brings little that is new in terms of example and principles, because all that it represents was already in place in Chile thirty-seven years ago."

In addition to such expressions of support, the Chilean Ministry of Foreign Relations reported to the Congress that "it views with great satisfaction" current developments in France.[3] However, the true republican posture of Chile—as viewed by the conservative government, the Catholic Church, and segments of the traditional oligarchy—became evident when various warnings and critiques about French events were expressed a few days later. When news arrived about the proletarian revolution of June in Paris, a virulent counterrevolutionary discourse took hold of Chilean opinion.[4] This dismissive attitude about the French '48 continued unabated for years.

And yet the enthusiasm for the revolutions of '48 remained strong among liberal (*pipiolo*) youth and—we may assume—some well-informed artisans. Proof of this can be found in the characteristics of the soon to be established Sociedad de la Igualdad [Society of Equality], especially during its early period. In agreement with historians who believe that the revolution of 1789 was important only much later and only at the level of ideas,[5] and that the revolution of 1830 was largely ignored, I argue that the European events of 1848 had a profound impact on the politics and society of mid-nineteenth-century Chile. I also contend that it had lasting consequences for Chilean history in the form of actual institutions and values.

What did the revolutionary movements of 1848 in Europe represent? The subject is large and complex, but one can approach it from a long-term perspective. The movements seem to be a return to the social and political forms of an emerging modernity, after they were temporarily crushed by the Restoration and the new international order inaugurated by the Congress of Vienna. Its central motifs were still those of the 1789–99 Revolution: political liberalism, nationalism, egalitarianism, rationalism, the imposition of a republican form of government, freedom of the press, secularization, an end to the remnants of feudalism, and an end to the institution of monarchy. But it was also (at least for some revolutionary segments) about the realization of new ideas: utopian socialism, social Catholicism, Romantic and messianic populism, and even an early form of positivism.[6] These ideas were present for decades, but they burst into the open in 1848. They had made an appearance in the revolution of 1830, growing stronger in European consciousness in the ensuing years, particularly among the intellectual elites, because they seemed to reflect the times and offer a better future not only for their respective societies but also for humanity.

It should be understood, then, that when I refer to the '48 and its influence, I mean more than the specific upheaval of February and the subsequent months. I also take into account the spirit and the feeling that preceded it for quite some time. It was an outlook that may not have been that of the majority of Europeans, not even of the majority of the intellectual elite, but one that was certainly adopted by significant groups that would become strong in the future. This was demonstrated by the subsequent history of Europe (and of France, which was at the crest of the revolutionary wave), to the point that several authors regard the '48 as the "axis" of the political evolution of Europe in the nineteenth century.[7] I will discuss this issue in more detail below.

: : :

The revolutions of 1848 constituted a European phenomenon, but France was the first and main theater of action.
This is the reason for its enormous influence in Chile, given
the importance of French culture in the society of the period, going back to independence and perhaps earlier.

Chile's national culture at the time of independence, as
was the case with society in general, was poor though rela-
tively homogeneous. There were marked distinctions of
class, but the differences in culture among classes were not so
sharp. On the contrary, there were significant commonalties,
to the point that different social groups shared a fairly simi
lar outlook: The transcendent view of human existence,
based on Catholicism, was the same and had great influence
on daily life. It was an omnipresent religiosity, of a Triden-
tine character, which was typical of the "Jesuit culture" of
Spanish America at the time.[8] The Jesuits had been expelled
from Spain and the colonies in 1767, but their influence,
which they had exercised for centuries, persisted.

Still, there were some important differences between the
culture of the oligarchy and that of the mestizo majority.
That of the former—also an ethnically mixed group—was
somewhat more rationalist and modern; its use of language,
basic arithmetic, weights and measures, social and economic
formulas, and money were of European origin; so were its
clothing and its taste (however dated) in art and architec-
ture. Some members of the oligarchy, especially males, were
highly educated. Colonial Chile had several institutions of
higher education and even a university, the University of San

Felipe, which had four faculties and granted more than three hundred doctoral degrees.[9]

Little is known about the culture of the great rural majority in the early nineteenth century, and that is certainly an important gap. But the developments that concern us here took place in a predominantly urban environment and were embraced by a small oligarchy. Therefore, we are talking mostly about the urban culture of the first half of the century.[10]

A new culture arrived in Chile during the late eighteenth century. I refer to the Enlightenment, a trend which, however modestly, reached the upper crust of Chilean society. It was a Catholic version of the Enlightenment, conveyed through imperial Spain and through such Spanish scholars as Benito Jerónimo Feijoo and Pedro Rodríguez de Campomanes. The French Enlightenment also arrived in distant Chile through the books that a few Creoles brought back with them after a European tour and, to a lesser extent, by a number of vessels passing through the Pacific Ocean. This is how they managed to elude the civil and ecclesiastical censorship. Such books included those of the Spanish authors already mentioned, in addition to the *Encyclopédie*, as well as works by Diderot, d'Alembert, Montesquieu, Rousseau, Helvétius, Raynal, Holbach, and Buffon.[11]

At first, these works attacking colonialism, absolutism, and the Catholic Church had little, if any, influence. This was due in part to their limited numbers (no more than two copies of the *Encyclopédie* arrived in Chile) and in large measure to the tiny number of people with enough education to read or understand them. The problem was compounded by the fact that many of these works were written in French, which even fewer people could read. However, the receptivity to the eighteenth-century trends increased with the independence of the United States and, subsequently, with the crisis precipitated by Napoleon's invasion of Spain (1808), which resulted in both the installation of the Cortes and the Regency representing the people of Spain along with its Spanish-American provinces.

It is quite possible that the influence of Enlightenment ideas was not the main motive for the Creoles' decision to seek independence from Spain. But once the process began, Creoles embraced those political ideas in order to legitimize the emerging republican order. The Chilean press of the period published, nearly verbatim, fragments of the *Social Contract*, the *Spirit of the Laws*, and the Constitution of the United States.[12] The ideas they contained were embraced by the Chilean-educated elite during the first republican governments. Also, the artistic and literary models of liberal, Romantic, and bourgeois Europe were highly admired and accepted, especially by the young, as a counterpoint to traditional Hispanic culture.

How did the preponderance of non-Hispanic Europeans, and especially the French, become established in Chile? It was a generalized phenomenon, but in Chile it was facilitated by some specific circumstances. Already in 1822, Bernardo O'Higgins, in his position of supreme director of the nation, hired European professors, including a Frenchman, Joseph Dauxion de Lavisse, to oversee the botanical garden in Chile. Another favorable condition was that, beginning in 1825, several upper-class youth traveled to France for a course of "studies," aided in no small measure, at least initially, by the French government's offer of free sea travel. It was the Baron de Mackau who initiated this program after visiting Chile in 1823. This is how, on January 16, 1825, the first group of Chileans departed for Paris on board the *Moselle*, a French warship en route to Le Havre. According to Vicente Pérez Rosales, they included "Santiago Rosales, Manuel Solar, the four Jaraquemada brothers (Lorenzo, Ramón, Manuel, and Miguel), the brothers Antonio and José de la Lastra, José Manuel Ramírez, my brother Ruperto, and me." Later, they were joined by Lorenzo, Calixto, and Víctor Guerrero, Rafael Santiago and José María Larraín Moxó, Bernardo, Domingo, Alonso, and Nicasio Toro, Manuel Izquierdo, Manuel Talavera, José Luis Borgoño, Ramón Undurraga, and Miguel Ramírez. Altogether, the group of young upper-class Chileans in Paris reached about twenty-six. They all enrolled in the Spanish-American school run by Manuel Silvela.[13]

As Pérez Rosales tells us, upon their return these *afrancesados* [francophiles], as they came to be called, brought books, art, furniture, and a deep admiration for French culture. Referring to this French fad, Simon Collier states that "the newspaper press of the 1820s, the period when political philosophizing flourished most richly, quoted an impressive range of thinkers. It would be nearly impossible to list them all, but the ten most popular authors—to judge from the number of times their names were invoked or their works quoted—were Montesquieu, Bentham, Constant, Rousseau, Voltaire, Filangieri, Mably, Paine, De Pradt, and Destutt de Tracy." That is, seven of these were French. As Collier adds, "The commanding position of Montesquieu can hardly be disputed," and yet the Creoles "took from him what they wanted and ignored the contradictory elements of his theory."[14]

The cultural renewal of the 1820s received additional impetus from initiatives of the war of independence (1810–17) and the O'Higgins administration (1817–23), such as the foundation of the National Library (1813), schools like the Instituto Nacional (1813), and the publication of several papers (more than ten between 1823 and 1829), although many did not last long.[15] Some philanthropic societies were modeled after those of the Enlightenment, such as the Society of Friends of Humankind (1826).

According to historian Julio Heise, the years 1810 to 1830 in Chile were a period of "political formation and learning. . . . Chileans lived in an era of transition in which the great principles that sustained the colonial period lost their prestige and power in the face of new ideals that had increasing relevance and authority. The value system that disciplined colonial existence lost its hold, but the new values that would replace it had not yet taken root."[16] In my judgment, this is a good characterization of the cultural-intellectual evolution of the period.

The new values, however, did eventually establish firm roots, due in no small measure to the educational efforts of both liberal (*pipiolo*) and conservative (*pelucón*) administrations. When the *pelucón* administrations ended in 1861, there were 911 schools, 648 of which were state or municipal schools, with an enrollment of more than 43,000 students.[17] According to a sociological study conducted in 1961, 10.9 percent of the school-age population was enrolled in primary schools. That same year, according to the national census, literacy had reached 17 percent.[18]

With regards to secondary education, the Instituto Nacional was the key institution. Eighty percent of the people who led Chile from 1830 to 1891 were educated in its classrooms. But in addition to the Instituto, there were a number of state schools in the provinces as well as private schools in Santiago and elsewhere. By 1861, there were eighteen state schools enrolling 2,500 students and sixty-three private schools with 3,800 students.[19]

But the most impressive cultural and educational development of the period was the foundation of the University of Chile in 1842. Following the model of the Institut de France, the Chilean institution was a deliberating, advising academic body that had the express responsibility of supervising national education. Until 1851, higher professional fields were taught at the Instituto Nacional. The various activities and functions of the university—the granting of degrees, the meetings and reports of the faculty, and the publication of the *Anales de la Universidad de Chile*—constituted a major contribution to the dissemination of knowledge and culture.[20]

:::

The cultural predominance of France declined somewhat with the emergence of the conservative, or *pelucón*, governments in 1831. This was the result not of a loss of prestige on the part of France but rather of the appeal of other European models, combined with a return to more traditional values.

In fact, France continued to be imitated, especially by young aristocrats. Francisco Bilbao, for instance, who was twenty years of age in 1843, sent a series of letters (some in French) to his friend Aníbal Pinto, the future president of Chile. This provides strong evidence of the predilection for things French on the part of the young. Few major French authors of the time fail to be mentioned in these letters.[21]

There are several factors that account for the diversification of European models and for the return to traditional values. First, the time that had elapsed since the war of independence (more than twelve years) had helped temper the anti-Spanish sentiment that had surely contributed to the adoption of French culture. Some elements of the Hispanic tradition were, in actions more than in discourse, once again considered valuable. The conservative victory in 1830 also represented a return to colonial social structures as well as to values and views so deeply rooted as to counterbalance the culture of rationalism and the Enlightenment.

There was another factor of critical if unintended importance: the 1829 arrival in Chile of Andrés Bello, who would become the undisputed center of intellectual life in Chile for more than thirty-five years. Bello occupied a number of important cultural and political positions. He was under-secretary of the Ministry of Foreign Relations (1829–52); principal writer and editor of *El Araucano*, the official paper (1830–53); the architect of the Chilean Civil Code (1841–55); and rector of the University of Chile (1843–65). Bello was also the respected mentor of an entire generation that included erudite scholars such as Diego Barros Arana and political firebrands such as Francisco Bilbao. Bello, who was born in Venezuela, had manifested a scholarly inclination since his youth.[22] In London, where he lived from 1810 to 1829, he acquired an impressive knowledge of philosophy, literature, law, philology, grammar, and several other fields. In 1829, he was hired by the liberal government of Chile. He also wrote several erudite works.[23] Highly influenced by the Scottish School of Common Sense, Bello was politically a liberal, both moderate and pragmatic. Committed as he was to order, Bello was an essential pillar of the conservative governments from 1830 to the 1860s. He was convinced that the generation nurtured by Portales represented the best political option for Chile.

The arrival of Bello strengthened the links between the Chilean educated elite and high European culture that included but was not restricted to France. Bello himself knew it well, but he admired British thought and institutions even more. He also had a profound knowledge of Spanish cultural traditions, which he promoted in language and literature.

And yet Bello was not the only highly learned foreigner in Chile at the time. After 1830, many European scholars and scientists as well as numerous Spanish Americans (mainly Argentine) arrived. The latter fled dictatorial persecution in their own countries and usually possessed a higher level of learning than was common in Santiago.[24]

Among the immigrant European intellectuals in Chile, there were several who were French but many who were not. Those of French origin included Claudio Gay, a naturalist and the first author of a Chilean physical and political history of Chile written in the republican period; the physician Lorenzo Sazié; the painter Raymond Monvoisin; the geologist Amadeo Pissis; and the architect François Brunet de Baines. Those of other European origin included the Polish Ignacio Domeyko, author of several works of geology, mineralogy, and education; the German botanist Rodulfo Phillipi; the Spanish mathematician Antonio Gorbea; the painters Mauricio Rugendas, German, and Alejandro Cicarelli, Italian; and the Spanish publishers and printers Santos Tornero and Narciso Desmadryl. These intellectuals contributed significantly to a Chilean cultural environment that, incidentally, had already been enhanced, if not shaken, by José Joaquín de Mora, a Spanish educator, literary scholar, and philosopher.

Among the Spanish Americans, one must not fail to mention Domingo Faustino Sarmiento, educator and polymath, Juan Bautista Alberdi, Bartolomé Mitre, Vicente Fidel López, Esteban Echeverría, Domingo de Oro, Gabriel Ocampo, Juan María Gutiérrez, and others. All of them were familiar with the political literature that emerged from the revolutionary cycle of 1830 in Europe, which passed almost unnoticed in Chile, but that made a strong impact in Argentina.[25] Sarmiento and Mitre later became presidents of their country. One must also mention the Colombian Juan García del Río and the Venezuelan Simón Rodríguez, who had been Simón Bolívar's mentor and who was familiar with the views of Robert Owen and perhaps even of Fourier and Saint-Simon.[26] Both the European and Spanish-American intellectuals resided in Chile for long periods, and some stayed there permanently.

Many of these foreigners, including Andrés Bello, were people of liberal inclinations. But they collaborated with the conservative governments out of economic necessity, like Sarmiento, although in some cases they did it out of conviction. This did not prevent them from making significant contributions, many associated with the values of modernity, to the Chilean cultural environment.

The manifestations of the new cultural climate were soon apparent. In 1842, a group of young liberal members of the Santiago oligarchy created the Sociedad Literaria. The most outstanding included Francisco Bilbao, José Victorino Lastarria, Jacinto Chacón, Juan N. Espejo, Eusebio Lillo, Juan Bello, Aníbal Pinto, and Santiago Lindsay. Many of them would bring new forms of social and cultural activity to the country. They were first "Chilean Girondins," and some would later be statesmen, including Aníbal Pinto, who served as president of Chile from 1876 to 1881. Also in 1842, three literary journals were published.[27] More appeared in the following years.

Simultaneously, an increasing number of books arrived from Europe, especially those representing the great movement of Romanticism. Victor Hugo, Chateaubriand, Lamartine, de Musset, and George Sand were among the French, but the works of Lord Byron, Walter Scott, Goethe, Larra, Espronceda, and Zorrilla were among the most popular, too. Encina asserts, with his usually mysterious command of sources, that Victor Hugo, Lamartine, and Chateaubriand were the writers most read by Chileans.[28]

It is important to note that more readers preferred to follow the Romantic *folletines*, which inundated Chile at the time, than to read "serious" literature. The most popular French authors of these folletines were Dumas père and

Eugène Sue. The great majority of the papers of the day published their works in sequential chapters that appeared daily. Even *El Amigo del Pueblo*, a short-lived revolutionary newspaper of the Society of Equality, published Dumas' *El collar de la reina*.[29] Between 1848 and 1851, other Chilean newspapers printed the following works by this author under the Spanish titles of *Los tres mosqueteros, Pablo Jones, El Conde de Montecristo, El caballero d'Harmental, Veinte años después, Los cuarenta y cinco, La dama de Monsoreau, Las dos Dianas, La guerra de las mujeres, La reina Margarita, El caballero de la casa roja, El vizconde de Bragelonne,* and *Angel Pitou*. Eugène Sue's novels were translated as *El judío errante, Los misterios de París, Matilde, Plik y Plok, Los siete pecados capitales, Teresa Dunoyer,* and *El castillo del diablo*.[30] According to Sarmiento, by 1849 thirty editions of *Los misterios de París* had been published. He also stated that "the novels published as folletines . . . number in the millions!"[31] But this is evidently an exaggeration. There were many British and Spanish folletines, but the French were overwhelmingly ahead of the others.

During this period, there was also a significant presence of political and philosophical literature: Herder, Cousin, Quinet, Lamennais, and the Utopian Socialists Fourier, Owen, and Blanc. It appears that Fourier was known in Chile by 1845,[32] but there is conclusive evidence that Francisco Bilbao sent translations of his writings to Chile in 1849, which were promptly published by the newspaper *El Progreso*.[33]

Historian Hernán Ramírez Necochea identified a bookstore catalog that listed the following titles in 1850: Louis Blanc's *L'Organisation du Travail* (Bruxelles, 1845); Pierre Joseph Proudhon's *Système de Contradictions Économiques* and

Philosophie de la misère (Paris, 1846), and, without indication of author, *Doctrine de Saint-Simon* (Bruxelles, 1831).[34] In 1844, a printer in Concepción published Lamennais' *El libro del pueblo*.[35] In 1848, the Imprenta Europea of Valparaíso published a pamphlet entitled *El socialismo, derecho al trabajo*, which was most likely derived from Louis Blanc.[36] It is almost certain that there were many other book imports, and even Chilean editions, by utopian socialists and Catholics. Many had been available in Spanish since the 1830s, most notably Lamennais' *Paroles d'un croyant*, translated as *Palabras de un creyente*.[37] At any rate, by 1850 the names of Saint-Simon and his followers, Louis Blanc and Fourier, were widely known in Santiago and were identified with revolution, social redemption, and "immorality."[38]

French influence in matters literary and political was predominant in the years after 1830, especially through the folletines, but it was balanced by the influence of other European areas. In historiography, however, French influence was particularly strong, thanks in many ways to Andrés Bello. He engaged in two major polemics on historiography: the first with José Victorino Lastarria, who was influenced by the interpretive historiography typical of the Enlightenment, and the second with Jacinto Chacón, a professor at the Instituto Nacional and a friend of Lastarria, who in the view of Bello also held outdated historiographical views. Bello's comments on the historical essays of Lastarria appeared in 1844 and 1847.[39] The polemics with Chacón took place in early 1848.[40]

Bello's rebuttal was memorable: he defended the thesis that in order to do good history one needed first to establish the facts and only then engage in interpretation. In the process, he provided abundant examples from the French Romantic School. In particular, he used as examples Barante's *Historia de los duques de Borgoña;* Augustin Thierry's *Historia de la conquista de Inglaterra por los Normandos;* Guizot's *Historia de la civilización europea;* and works by Michelet, Thiers, and Tocqueville. In essence, the most formidable intellectual presence of Chile during the period enshrined the methods of French historiography. This fact, combined with the historicist character of Romantic literature, either "serious" or in the form of folletines (especially the writings of Dumas père), had a direct bearing on the sociocultural phenomenon that occurred in Chile beginning in early 1848: the enormous success and influence of Alphonse de Lamartine's *Histoire des Girondins,* which was preceded by the fame it achieved in Paris.

:::

The first copies of the *Histoire des Girondins* arrived in Valparaíso in February 1848, where they sold at the exorbitant price of six ounces of gold. Vicuña Mackenna tells us that this "immortal work enjoyed an immense popularity in Chile, and especially in Santiago, which no other book had, or perhaps ever will."[41] From the middle of 1848, a kind of cult developed around this work, which was discussed and analyzed in evening meetings in private homes or during the workday in the editing room of the liberal paper *El Progreso.*[42] This was, of course, yet another practice copied from

France.[43] Why did the *Histoire* achieve such success? As I mentioned, it was to a great extent due to the impact of the book in France itself.

When Alphonse de Lamartine published the first volume of his *Histoire des Girondins* in 1847, France fell under some kind of a spell. The day of the book's appearance, Lamartine wrote to a friend: "I have gambled my fortune, my literary renown, and my political future today on a single card. I have won. My editors tell me that they have never seen a success like this." It was the pure truth. While critics disapproved of the work, the publishers could not keep up with the colossal demand. "Women and youth are with me," wrote the delighted Lamartine. "As for the rest, I can do without them." When a few days later he asked Alexandre Dumas about the possible reasons for such triumph, Dumas responded with a resounding compliment: "Because you have raised history to the level of the novel."[44]

And yet the *Histoire* is bad history, perhaps the worst there is. Not only does it make no attempt to hide the republican ideological bias that inspires it, but it is also a badly researched work. The author's imagination filled the "gaps" in the story he told. At the same time, and despite its title, *Histoire*, the book is actually a history of the French Revolution up to 9 Thermidor and the death of Robespierre. In addition, Lamartine confuses dates, omits subjects and facts that he disliked, and even invents some episodes. His purpose was to glorify the Girondins in general (whose role, according to the majority of historians, was dubious at best) and Pierre Vergniaud in particular. The latter was transformed into a tragic and exceptional figure. Lamartine invented a "last supper" that did not exist, yet it was painted as if it did by Raymond Monvoisin, as Vicuña Mackenna tells us in this book. With Vergniaud dead, Lamartine transferred his admiration to Robespierre without regard to some contradictions. In another example, he narrates a long story about Charlotte Corday, about whom little or nothing is known.[45] Godechot summarizes his opinion about the Girondins as follows: "Lamartine is frequently content with mediocre information, and uses his imagination to twist it and adulterate it."[46]

In sum, the book is another example of how bad history, when it is imaginative and passionate, can enjoy tremendous success. What is most interesting and curious is that the popularity of the book in France would be reproduced in Chile. It is highly probable that the book's fame may have preceded its actual arrival in Valparaíso in February 1848, that is, shortly after the French publication.

: : :

The fame that preceded the arrival of Lamartine's book, however, is not sufficient to explain its astonishing success in Chile or the fact that it unleashed a veritable frenzy among the young. It was the revolutionary climate of France itself in 1848 (what we might call "the culture of '48"), which caught people's imagination in the remote yet admiring country of South America. Let us then provide a brief view of France in the 1840s and the principal causes of the revolutionary upheaval, for this is quite useful for understanding the Chilean case.

Louis-Philippe d'Orléans had assumed power in Paris in 1830. His mandate was marked initially by the desire for change and the triumph of new economic, social, and political forms of modernity. He was a king born of revolution, initially seen with distrust if not hostility by conservative Legitimists, and with great hopes by progressive groups. Soon after his installation, Louis-Philippe showed an inclination to establish alliances with the high bourgeoisie and even some supporters of the ancien régime. Heavily influenced by François Guizot, the king became more and more authoritarian, seeking to make his country a hierarchical society governed by an elite of wealth and intellect, buttressed by a restricted suffrage. But he clashed against powerful social forces. We have already mentioned the Legitimists, who were somewhat mollified by the authoritarian path followed by the regime. That very change of course pitted him against republican and progressive forces that felt understandably betrayed. These predominantly liberal groups were soon joined by others: utopian socialists, social Catholics, proto-anarchists, carbonari, and communists, as well as by the more diffuse proletariat that grew out of French industrialization.

During the 1840s, these groups—which had nearly complete control of the press—were joined by large segments of the intellectual bourgeoisie, as well as the powerful French Catholic Church. The latter institution had never seen the Voltairean king Louis-Philippe with much sympathy, but had managed to reach an accommodation with the regime. By the middle of the decade, however, the Church turned against it in protest against the secularizing educational policies promoted by Guizot.[47]

This political situation was also reflected in the ideological sphere. Beginning in the 1830s, France witnessed the consolidation of an ideological current that promoted republican, populist, and democratic views and embraced social utopias while upholding the legacies of the French Revolution of 1789. In the years prior to the fall of Louis-Philippe, this intellectual climate had extended to the entire country.[48] As Tocqueville put it, "The intention was to destroy inequalities of wealth; level the oldest inequality, that between men and women. Remedies were proposed against the evils of work, etc. . . . In addition, a romantic and revolutionary vocabulary developed that gave new resonance to words such as people, fraternity, republic, and equality."[49]

Thus, if in the beginning these views were confined to small circles that espoused complex utopian ideas, increasingly they reached the middle class and the popular sectors. Much of this happened as a consequence of the larger political discontent mentioned above, compounded by scandals and government errors, and the severe economic crisis of 1847. Both the middle class and the popular sectors found common grounds in their aspirations for political democracy and socioeconomic improvement. Therefore, and in spite of the fact that the movement against the July Monarchy was led by bourgeois intellectuals and politicians like Thiers, Lamartine, and Ledru-Rollin, one might agree with Maurice Agulhon when he states that "since early 1848, the agreement between the popular movement and the utopians seemed imminent" and that "the socialism of the intellectuals, which in 1833 was little more than a small sectarian preference, became a central element of politics."[50]

The most influential utopian—and republican—socialist of the French '48 appears to have been Louis Blanc, as became clear after February of that year. But even the followers of Saint-Simon, Fourier, Proudhon, and other utopian socialists entered the political arena to "demand universal suffrage, proclaim popular infallibility, and celebrate the merits of the great predecessors of '93."[51] This political and ideological encounter between utopian socialism and republican and democratic—or populist—intellectual trends was joined by a third current in the 1840s: Christianity. This encounter had deeper roots than that generated by the period's political and educational debates.

The "Lamennais episode," which would become so influential in Chile, had been the first of these encounters. It was followed by other events that included the participation of priests (like Jules Pautet, Tranchant, and Clavel de Saint-Geniez) and lay Catholics (like Alphonse Esquiroz), to the point that this became a recurring phenomenon. References were made to "the proletarian from Nazareth" and even to "the sansculotte Jesus."[52] As Georges Weill has stated, "The French clergy embraced liberty on the eve of a revolution that would then attempt to extend it to all."[53] This encounter, again, had deeper roots than simply conjunctural reasons. Moreover, the approach of utopian socialists to Christianity makes a good deal of sense in the context of Romanticism, as shown by such figures as Pecquer, Buchez, and Leroux. Pierre Leroux is a very good example: Former

Carbonari and former Saint-Simonian, he stated in 1848 that "Jesus Christ is the greatest economist, and there is no true economic science without him."[54]

Cuvillier gives us the following explanation for the attitude of the utopian leftist intellectuals: "Beyond the French Revolution, the men of '48 wanted to trace the ideas of equality and fraternity to their very source. The majority of them found that source in Christianity. This is what Buchez had asserted in his renowned *Parliamentary History of the French Revolution*, and what his disciples at the newspaper *L'Atelier* believed."[55]

And yet the Paris of the 1840s was more than a politico-ideological cauldron. It was also a cultural center of great brilliance. Among the literary people there were Hugo, Lamartine, Dumas, Georges Sand, and Balzac. In the field of philosophy, Comte had published *The Course of Positive Philosophy* in 1842. In history, Michelet had been publishing his *History of France* since 1833. This was also the time when the works of Buchez, Roux, Thierry, Quinet, and Guizot appeared. Tocqueville had published his *Democracy in America* in 1835. In music, Berlioz and Chopin were actively composing and the painters Delacroix, Corot, Courbet, Ingres, and Daumier were at the height of their creative work. The press was flourishing thanks to the talented writers Armand Carrel, Armand Marrast, Godefroy Cavaignac, Flocon, Considerant, Cormenin, Ledru-Rollin, and many others.

In a different area, openly at first and clandestinely after their prohibition, there was a resurgence of the forms of political association that had emerged during the French Revolution. In the 1830s, several clubs modeled after those of the

1789–94 period had been created: Aide-toi, le Ciel t'Aidera, Association de la Presse, Association pour l'Éducation du Peuple, Société des Amis du Peuple, and others. They were structured in the form of cells, forming a territorial network, and followed common principles, programs, and rules. They were persecuted after the attempted coup of 1839,[56] when they fragmented and went underground. They survived and continued to function until they emerged again on the eve of the revolution of February 1848. During the last few months of the Louis-Philippe government, and especially after its fall, these networks of republican societies or clubs flourished in Paris and throughout France, becoming vehicles for modern political ideas and republican propaganda.[57]

All of this suggests that, in the 1840s, a climate of renewal and an aspiration to social reform prevailed in Europe in general and France in particular. This process resumed the modernizing impulse that had been interrupted during the Restoration. Now that the penuries of the French Revolution had receded from memory, its ideological legacies appeared once again to offer a path of hope, enriched this time by multiple new ideological trends. This modernizing republican and democratic vision was characterized, in its philosophical and existential dimensions, by rationalism, individualism, and a liberal conception of what society ought to be.

Hence the revolutions of 1848—despite their utopian socialist features—were essentially liberal. This liberalism was, at this time in Europe, a predominantly revolutionary doctrine. The one exception to this is Great Britain, where liberal conceptions of man and society had long been a part of national culture and had become a part of bourgeois tradition. In France, in contrast, where political liberalism had been strangled by Napoleon, the Restoration, and Louis-Philippe, and where economic liberalism had never established firm roots, liberal ideas now acquired an innovative, indeed revolutionary character.[58]

In Chile, the impressive French intellectual ferment of the years 1844–49 had the effect of renewing and augmenting the admiration of the new generation for France, a country that became the model in matters well beyond the intellectual. Historian Jaime Eyzaguirre states, quite correctly in my opinion, that in this *quarante-huitard* environment, "young Chileans viewed not only liberal ideas as a panacea . . . but also lived them with their sights fixed on Paris, the place that dictated, without appeal, their manner of thinking, dressing, and eating."[59] Vicuña Mackenna, a witness to this phenomenon, stated that "both society and nation were extremely receptive to the spirit of '48."[60]

The young francophiles of the Chilean oligarchy constituted a brilliant generation. Vicuña Mackenna gives their names, some of which have already been mentioned: "Lastarria, the Amunátegui brothers, Benavente, Santa María, Father Salas, Tocornal, Concha y Toro, Sanfuentes, Espejo, Blanco Cuartín, the three Matta brothers, R. Vial, Felipe Herrera, Eusebio Lillo, Ambrosio Montt, Francisco Marín, Mercedes Marín, Pedro Gallo, Jacinto Chacón, Santiago Lindsay, Víctor and Pío Varas, Francisco and Manuel Bilbao, the three brothers Blest Gana, Isidoro Errázuriz," etc.[61] To this list one should add Federico Errázuriz, Vicente Reyes, Manuel Guerrero, Manuel Recabarren, Juan Bello, Eduardo de la Barra, Marcial González, and Santiago Arcos, in addition to Vicuña Mackenna himself, the child prodigy of the group and the author of the book presented here.

The revolutionary seed of the French '48 found fertile ground among these young men who, along with the artisans of Santiago, became the principal actors of the Chilean '48. From this group, two presidents of the nation would emerge in the second half of the nineteenth century: Federico Errázuriz Zañartu and Domingo Santa María; many more senators and cabinet ministers; two defeated presidential candidates, Vicente Reyes and Benjamín Vicuña Mackenna; the best Chilean novelist of the nineteenth century, Alberto Blest Gana,[62] and the most important liberal ideologue of the period, José Victorino Lastarria. In fact, most if not all of the names mentioned above became notable personalities in Chile's public life.

But let us return to the *Histoire des Girondins* and its influence in Chile. After the news of the February 1848 revolution became known, the idolatry for the figures of Lamartine's work was such that many liberal youth identified themselves with, and took the names of, various Girondin or Jacobin personalities: Lastarria became Brissot; Bilbao, a fiery speaker, became Vergniaud after his return to Chile in 1850; Manuel Recabarren became Barbaroux; Juan Bello and Rafael Vial became Ducos and Boyer-Fonfrède; Domingo Santa María chose Louvet as his model. There was also a Pétion, some Lameth brothers, a Danton, a Saint-Just, and a Robespierre. Eusebio Lillo, a poet-musician who would later be the chief writer for the paper *El Amigo del Pueblo,* could not resist becoming Rouget de Lisle. Santiago Arcos became

Marat.[63] These are all members of the group that Vicuña Mackenna christened as "the Chilean Girondins," even though he made it clear that when he talked about "Girondins" he referred really to the actors of the French Revolution. In reality, Robespierre (Francisco Marín), Danton (Pedro Ugarte), Saint-Just (Manuel Bilbao), and Marat (Santiago Arcos) were never Girondins. On the contrary, they were their worst enemies. Vicuña Mackenna called them "Girondins" because he admired the period as presented by Lamartine, rather than because of the historical figures whose names they assumed.

:::

The political events of the year 1848 provided a favorable environment for the warm reception of Lamartine's *Histoire des Girondins* in Chile. After the fall of the moderate conservative Manuel Camilo Vial, Bulnes' minister of the interior and head of the cabinet, a highly authoritarian group entered the government, headed by Manuel Montt. The ranks of the liberals, who had become rather dormant during the tolerant years of the Bulnes administration (the exception being the repressive months before the presidential elections of 1846), began to show signs of revolutionary feeling. Even the grandees of the Santiago aristocracy voiced their discontent with the turn of events and formed the first Reform Club (Club de la Reforma) in Chilean history. The secretary of this club was Benjamín Vicuña Mackenna.

The young liberals just mentioned, the Chilean "Girondins," became the most militant group, rejecting the authoritarian conservatives now in charge of the government. The fact that they met in the offices of the newspaper *El Progreso* to read aloud Lamartine's book shows the extent of their Parisian inclinations. Georges Weill has described how the intellectual circles of the French republican party, toward the end of the July monarchy, met in the offices of the newspapers *Le National* and *La Réforme*, which became the main conspiratorial centers of the period. It was there, to a great extent, that the French '48 was conceived.[64]

Vicuña Mackenna was at the center of the Chilean circle of young Girondins, as part conspirator and part organizer. In his later works—including *Los Girondinos Chilenos*—he provided a somewhat detached, even sarcastic commentary on the people and situations confronted by this group. But there is more than a bit of guilt and emotional release in that approach, given the fact that he was one of the most enthusiastic members of the movement. It is certainly not true that he was, as historian Francisco Antonio Encina and others have described him, a congenital troublemaker. He was rather a romantic, a liberal, who showed some of the eccentric brilliance that ran in his family. He read voraciously and unsystematically, adored the theater, attended the sessions of Congress, and found time to debate, conspire, and even write his first journalistic article in the newspaper *La Tribuna* in 1849.

It is important to recall that the man who wrote *Los Girondinos Chilenos* in 1876 was a mature, if not old, Vicuña Mackenna. How much of the spirit of '48 was left in him? If one were to judge by the ironic detachment of his description, one would have to admit that not very much was. And yet he probably retained more than he let be known in *Los*

Girondinos. One could cite, for instance, his populist campaign for the presidency in 1876 and his "uncompromising" liberalism, which also characterized the Girondin generation when it reached maturity. This is the group that, once it became part of the government after 1870, implemented the "Liberal Republic" of Chile.

Even if by 1876 Vicuña Mackenna could smile at the revolutionary posturing of Chilean liberal youth during 1848, what had happened in the country in subsequent years demonstrated that the revolutionary spirit was very much alive. Specifically, this generation refused to accept the conservative and authoritarian Manuel Montt as the successor of Manuel Bulnes to the presidency of Chile. In part due to the ineffectiveness of the Reform Club, a more radical group emerged, the Society of Equality. This Society was founded by Santiago Arcos (Marat) on the model of a republican society that he had known in France, where he lived for most of his youth. In Chile, the Society grew rapidly. It was structured in the form of cells and had a progressive program of social and political reform.[65] On account of its structure, methods, and aims, it was in fact the first modern political party of Chile. It was also the first political organization to recruit followers among the artisans of Santiago and other members of the lower class. It is true that the Society emerged primarily in opposition to the candidacy of Montt, but its long-term objectives—however confusing—were much more ambitious: It sought profound social and economic changes in the country.

It is well worth quoting at length the statements of Santiago Arcos to the Reform Club in 1849. There he not only criticized their lack of efficacy but also advanced his notion, for the first time in Chile, of what constituted a modern club or political party:

> This reformist society will not achieve anything by collective rule, nor will the leaders implement a single plan if they are unable to keep it secret. Here we all want to know what the directorate did and will do in the future. The Club is not [a Masonic] lodge, but the leaders must maintain reserve, even secrecy, when they deem it important. We have already deliberated; it is now time for action. We must see the directorate as three bodies animated by a single spirit. . . .
>
> The French clubs comply with the spirit of their directorates. The English word for *club* has the connotation of sphere or circle. . . .
>
> A political "club" represents the merging of several wills that form a single spirit in order to determine goals for the public good. Its action is extended to other related associations, and the [club] communicates with them through channels that are continuously open. . . .
>
> Discord is the worst ill that can affect a "club." Discord makes it impotent, and thus it approaches dissolution just like any other organism in nature that loses the equilibrium of life. . . .
>
> A political club is the synthesis of a generalized idea. . . .
>
> A corporation needs to become even more concentrated, in order to create a spirit that will represent it, direct it, and make decisions, under the name of 'directorate.' . . .
>
> In Chile there are no political clubs. . . .
>
> In France the members of a club submit their will to a directorate, which acts according to its own judgment.[66]

This speech shows the disillusionment of the francophile Arcos, who had probably participated in a Parisian republican club, when looking at the loud but ineffective first reform club of Chile, an organization that was viewed with complete contempt by its *pelucón* enemies. As Vicuña Mackenna states, Arcos viewed the Reform Club as a place "attended primarily and routinely by . . . those gentlemen who lead an idle life in Santiago, as is common among landowners who rise and go to bed early and earnestly only in the countryside."[67] At the same time, he understood that there was a different attitude among the liberal, intellectual, and francophile youth—the Chilean Girondins. Barros Arana clarifies this point: "Arcos understood early on that the country could not expect much from [the old *pipiolos*]; he also realized that some younger members were animated by ardent and noble sentiments. . . . Arcos identified them as Eusebio Lillo, Manuel Recabarren, and Benjamín Vicuña Mackenna. He also counted Manuel Guerrero and the musician José Zapiola who, in addition to maintaining their youthful commitment to liberal ideas, had also suffered persecution and exile because of their beliefs."[68]

The main purpose of Arcos was to terminate the informal and ineffective form of political association represented by the Reform Club and replace it with a formal and modern one. His words did not hide the origin of his ideas, and even the words he used reveal the model he proposed. As Maurice Agulhon states in *Le Cercle dans la France Bourgeoise, 1810–1848*, "Everyone knows that this word [*circle*] is the French equivalent of the English *club*."[69] Undoubtedly, the semi-French Arcos hoped to transform the Chilean Reform Club into a revolutionary club or circle like those of the France of Louis-Philippe d'Orléans. He was providing the model for what would become the second Club de la

Reforma (1868–71), the future Radical Party of the 1860s,[70] and then every other political party until the emergence of socialist groups after the 1920s. In short, he was announcing and promoting the transformation of existing forms of political association in Chile, to make these new organizations similar to the republican clubs and political parties of Louis-Philippe's France.

The Society of Equality did not last long; indeed, it was outlawed in November 1850. Thus, the first lasting new form of political association was the Radical Party. Its founder, Manuel Antonio Matta, played the same role of Arcos in creating the Society of Equality. Matta had left for Europe with his brother and Francisco Bilbao in late 1844. When he returned in 1849, Matta did not join the ranks of the Chilean Girondins. He demonstrated little interest in the activities of the Society of Equality or in the political events of the momentous 1850–51 period, that is, the Chilean '48. We do not know exactly why. It was only in 1855, when elected as congressman for Copiapó, that Matta showed himself to be a convinced liberal, republican, and democrat as well as a determined enemy of Manuel Montt's government. During the political upheavals of 1857, he and Vicuña Mackenna published the newspaper *La Asamblea Constituyente*. There he gathered a group of young liberals who became active within the Pipiolo Party (which we might now call "liberal") to oppose the Liberal-Conservative Fusion that emerged out of the crisis known as the Sacristán Affair.[71] Historians of the Radical Party agree that the group of doctrinaire and anticlerical members who would later become the core of the party, including Angel Custodio Gallo, Francisco Marín,

Justo Arteaga Alemparte, Luis Rodríguez Velasco, Santiago Cobo, Manuel Antonio and Guillermo Matta, had all belonged to or were direct descendants of the "liberal youth of Bulnes's time," that is, the Chilean Girondins.[72]

Despite his passive politics during 1850–51, Manuel Antonio Matta had assimilated the ideas and the spirit of the European '48. Unlike Arcos or Bilbao, he was able to organize, especially after his election to the Congress in 1855, a cohesive group that would carry and disseminate the legacies of that era. The name *radicals* was first given to them in the form of an adjective, that is, to designate the most extreme and uncompromising wing of the liberals (or those who were still *pipiolos*). The label was meant to describe their anticonservative attitudes in general and their anticlerical positions in particular. They were the true heirs of the Chilean Girondins.

—*Cristián Gazmuri*
—*translated by Iván Jaksić*

Notes

1. Benjamín Vicuña Mackenna, *Los Girondinos chilenos* (Santiago: Editorial Universitaria, 1989), 23. This work was originally published in the form of press articles that appeared in the newspapers *El Ferrocarril* and *La Patria* in 1876.

2. Jorge Edwards, "El decenio de Bulnes a través de los archivos del Quai d'Orsay," in *Boletín de la Academia Chilena de la Historia*, no. 74 (1966): 20.

3. The *Memoria Ministerial* appeared in *El Araucano*, no. 13, October 13, 1848.

4. Ignacio Muñoz D., "Análisis cuantitativo de la evolución del imaginario del sector aglutinado en torno a la Revista Católica," in *Nuestra Epoca,* September 1989, 22–40. *La Tribuna* was a conservative (*pelucón*) paper that represented the views of Manuel Montt and his supporters. This paper also reflected the changes described in the text. Another interesting account of the impact of the 1848 French revolution in Chile, and the reaction of the *pelucón* government, is Joseph Miran, *Un français au Chili* (Paris: Editions du CNRS, 1987), 49–50.

5. For instance, historian Francisco Encina asserts with the questionable modesty that was his signature that "when we re-create the reality of the period under the serene guidance of our contemporary minds, we can conclude by looking at the press and political pamphlets of the 1850–51 period that we are witnessing a form of collective madness." *Historia de Chile* (Santiago: Nascimento, 1951), 16:144.

6. A. Jardin and A. J. Tudesq, *La France des notables, 1815–1848,* Nouvelle Histoire de la France Contemporaine, no. 6 (Paris: Eds. du Seuil, 1973).

7. See, among others, Maurice Agulhon, *1848 ou l'Apprentisage de la République* (Paris: Eds. du Seuil, 1973).

8. Hernán Godoy Urzúa, *La cultura chilena* (Santiago: Editorial Universitaria, 1982), 99–148.

9. Walter Hanisch, "Del primer colegio de los jesuitas al Instituto Nacional (1653–1813)," *Boletín de la Academia Chilena de la Historia,* no. 68 (Semester I, 1963): 110–36; José Toribio Medina, *Historia de la Real Universidad de San Felipe de Santiago de Chile,* 2 vols. (Santiago: Sociedad Imprenta y Litografía Universo, 1928).

10. The subject still awaits a comprehensive treatment, but scholars Juan Uribe Echeverría, Ricardo Latcham, Mario Góngora, and Hernán Godoy Urzúa have treated various aspects of it.

11. See Miguel Luis Amunátegui, *Los precursores de la Independencia de Chile,* vol. 3 (Santiago: Imprenta Barcelona, 1909), and Cristián Gazmuri, "Ideas y libros políticos franceses en la

gestación de la Independencia de Chile," in Ricardo Krebs and Cristián Gazmuri, eds., *La revolución francesa y Chile* (Santiago: Editorial Universitaria, 1990), 151–78.

12. Raúl Silva Castro, *Prensa y periodismo en Chile (1812–1956)* (Santiago: Editorial del Pacífico, 1962), and Simon Collier, *Ideas and Politics of Chilean Independence, 1808–1833* (Cambridge: Cambridge University Press, 1967).

13. Vicente Pérez Rosales, *Recuerdos del pasado* (Buenos Aires: Francisco de Aguirre, 1971), 95–112. This source will soon appear in English in the Oxford Library of Latin America Series, with an introduction by Brian Loveman. See also the introduction of Guillermo Feliú Cruz to the *Diccionario del entrometido de Vicente Pérez Rosales* (Santiago: Difusión, 1946).

14. Collier, *Ideas and Politics*, 171–72.

15. Silva Castro, *Prensa*, chap. 2.

16. Quoted by Hernán Godoy in *La cultura chilena*, 256.

17. Fernando Campos Harriet, *Desarrollo educacional, 1810–1860* (Santiago: Andrés Bello, 1960), 26.

18. Eduardo Hamuy, *El problema educacional del pueblo de Chile* (Santiago: Editorial del Pacífico, 1961), 8.

19. Campos, *Desarrollo*, 79.

20. Simon Collier, "Evolución política, institucional, social y cultural de Chile entre 1829 y 1865," in *Bello y Chile*, 2 vols. (Caracas: La Casa de Bello, 1982), 1:46.

21. Francisco Bilbao to Aníbal Pinto, August 1848, in *Archivo Domingo Santa María*, Santiago de Chile, no. 00747.

22. At the age of nineteen, Bello accompanied Alexander von Humboldt during part of his research in Venezuela. See Oscar Sambrano Urdantea, "Cronología de Bello en Caracas," in *Bello y Caracas* (Caracas: La Casa de Bello, 1979), 95 ff.

23. See the biography by Miguel Luis Amunátegui, *Vida de don Andrés Bello* (Santiago: P. Ramírez, 1882). See also Iván Jaksić, *Andrés Bello: Scholarship and Nation-Building in Nineteenth-Century Latin America* (Cambridge: Cambridge University Press,

2001) and his edited volume, *Selected Writings of Andrés Bello*, published in the Oxford Library of Latin America series in 1997.

24. There are several studies of the impressive European and Spanish-American presence in Chile, beginning with the contemporary accounts of Diego Barros Arana, Benjamín Vicuña Mackenna, Isidoro Errázuriz, José Victorino Lastarria, José Joaquín Vallejo ("Jotabeche"), and others. More recently, a doctoral thesis has uncovered valuable new information: Roberto Hernández Ponce, "Sabios extranjeros en el desarrollo cultural de Chile" (Ph.D. diss., Universidad Católica de Chile, 1986).

25. The European revolutions of 1830 produced great agitation in the cultural and political circles of Argentina. As Norberto Pinilla explains, "From that date onwards, books by the following authors arrived: Hugo, Georges Sand, Saint-Beuve, Lamartine, Dumas, Delavigne (. . .) Villemain, Quinet, Michelet, Guizot, Lamennais, Cousin, Lerminier, Thiers, Nizard, and the German historian and philologist Niebuhr." See his *La generación chilena de 1842* (Santiago: Manuel Barros B., 1943), 77, where he cites Vicente Fidel López. Domingo Faustino Sarmiento, in his *Recuerdos de provincia* (1850), mentions Hugo, Dumas, Lamartine, Chateaubriand, Thiers, Guizot, Tocqueville, Lerminier, Jouffroy, and Cousin. We may assume that he was acquainted with these authors before his arrival in Chile in 1841.

26. José Victorino Lastarria, *Recuerdos literarios* (Santiago: Zig-Zag, 1968), 53. An English translation, edited by Frederick Nunn, *Literary Memoirs*, appeared in the Oxford Library of Latin America series in 2000.

27. Hernán Godoy, *La cultura chilena*, 312.

28. Encina, *Historia de Chile*, 12:476.

29. When *El Amigo del Pueblo* was closed on June 4, 1850, the successor newspaper, *La Barra*, continued the publication of Dumas's work.

30. A complete listing of the folletines published by the Chilean press between 1830 and 1890 is in María Carolina Roblero

A., *El folletín literario* (graduate thesis, Instituto de Historia, Universidad Católica de Chile, 1992).

31. Domingo Faustino Sarmiento, *Obras completas* (Santiago: Imprenta Gutenberg, 1885). These comments appeared in separate articles in the newspaper *La Crónica* in 1849. They are included in 2:336 ff. and 3:334–39.

32. Jaime Eyzaguirre, *Historia de Chile* (Santiago: Zig-Zag, 1973), 564.

33. *El Progreso*, May 2, 1849.

34. Hernán Ramírez Necochea, *Historia del movimiento obrero de Chile* (Santiago: LAR, 1986), 146.

35. H. F. de Lamennais, *El libro del pueblo* (Concepción: Imprenta del Instituto, 1844).

36. Ramón Briseño, *Estadística bibliográfica (1812–1876)* (Santiago: Biblioteca Nacional, 1965), 2:438.

37. We know that Mariano José de Larra translated the *Paroles d'un croyant* into Spanish in 1836. See J. Touchard, *Historia de las ideas políticas* (Madrid: Tecnos, 1981), 445. An anonymous presentation of the views of Fourier was translated in 1841 (Barcelona: J. Roger, 410 pp.). Lamennais's book appears to have been translated in London in 1834, that is, before Larra's translation. This is the edition that arrived in Chile. See María Eugenia Pinto and Patricia Arancibia, *La obra de pensadores europeos en la biblioteca del Instituto Nacional, 1861–1890, un estudio comparativo* (graduate thesis, Instituto de Historia, Universidad Católica de Chile, 1980), 220.

38. Diego Barros Arana, *Un decenio de la historia de Chile*, 2 vols. (Santiago: Imprenta, Litografía y Encuadernación Barcelona, 1913), 2:385–86.

39. *El Araucano*, November 8 and 15, 1844; *El Araucano*, January 7, 1847.

40. *El Araucano*, January 28, 1848 ("Modo de escribir la historia"), and February 14, 1848 ("Modo de estudiar la historia"). These articles appear in English in *Selected Writings of Andrés Bello*, 175–86.

41. Vicuña Mackenna, *Los Girondinos chilenos*, 31.

42. Ibid., 47.

43. Georges Weill, *Histoire du Parti Républicaine en France (1814–1870)* (Paris and Geneva: Ed. Ressources, 1980), chap. 6.

44. Cristián Gazmuri, "Los Girondinos chilenos y su época," introduction to Vicuña Mackenna, *Los Girondinos chilenos*, 7.

45. G. P. Gooch, *History and Historians in the Nineteenth Century* (Boston: Beacon Press, 1962), 215–16.

46. J. Godechot, *Las revoluciones* (Barcelona: Labor, 1981), 159.

47. Pierre Rosanvallon, *Le Moment Guizot* (Paris: Gallimard, 1985), chap. 7. See also Jacques Droz, *Europa, restauración y revolución, 1815–1848* (Madrid: Siglo XXI, 1974), chap. 5.

48. Jardin and Tudesq, *La France des notables*, 87–113 ("La vie intellectualle sous la restauration").

49. Quoted by J. C. Petitfils, *Los socialismos utópicos* (Madrid: Aldala, 1979), 158.

50. Maurice Agulhon, *Une ville ouvrière au temps du socialisme utopique: Toulon, 1815 à 1851* (Paris and The Hague: Mouton, 1970), 265.

51. Agulhon, quoted by Petitfils, *Los socialismos utópicos*, 163.

52. Jean Bruhat, "Le socialisme français de 1815 à 1848," in *Histoire générale du socialisme* (Vendôme: Presses Universitaires de France, 1972), 1:330–406.

53. Georges Weill, *Histoire du catholicisme libéral en France, 1848–1908* (Paris and Geneva: Ed. Ressources, 1970), 90.

54. Petitfils, *Los socialismos utópicos*, 168.

55. A. Cuvillier, *Hommes et idéologues de 1840* (Paris: L. Marcel Rivière, 1956), 240.

56. They were prohibited by article 291 of the Penal Code.

57. Maurice Agulhon, *1848 ou l'apprentisage*, and *The Republic in the Village* (Cambridge University Press and Eds. de la Maison des Sciences de L'Homme, 1981). See also J. Berthier et al., 1848, *Les Utopismes sociaux* (Paris: SEDES, 1981).

58. André Jardin, *Histoire du liberalisme politique* (Paris: Hachette, 1985), chap. 22.

59. Jaime Eyzaguirre, *Historia de Chile*, 564–65.

60. Vicuña Mackenna, *Los Girondinos chilenos*, 24.

61. Ibid., 7.

62. Blest Gana described the views and attitudes of the francophile Chilean youth in one of his major novels, *Martín Rivas* (1862). An English version was published in the Oxford Library of Latin America series, edited by Jaime Concha, in 2000.

63. Vicuña Mackenna, *Los Girondinos chilenos*, 53–63.

64. Georges Weill, *Histoire du Parti Républicaine*, chap. 6.

65. Cristián Gazmuri, *El '48 Chileno: Igualitarios, reformistas, radicales, masones, y bomberos*, 2d ed. (Santiago: Editorial Universitaria and Centro de Investigaciones Diego Barros Arana, 1998).

66. Antonio Iñíguez V., *Historia del período revolucionario chileno, 1848–1851* (Santiago: Imprenta del Comercio, 1902), 512–13.

67. Benjamín Vicuña Mackenna, *Historia de la jornada del 20 de abril de 1850* (Santiago: Rafael Jover, 1878), 26.

68. Barros Arana, *Un decenio*, 2:381.

69. Maurice Agulhon, *Le Cercle dans la France bourgeoise, 1810–1848* (Paris: Armand Colin, 1977).

70. The Radical Party was still in existence in Chile in 2001.

71. René León Echaiz, *Evolución histórica de los partidos políticos chilenos* (Santiago: Editorial del Pacífico, 1949), 58–59; Angel C. Espejo, *El Partido Radical, sus obras y sus hombres* (Santiago: Imprenta Esmeralda, 1912), 95–129; Yerko Koscina, *El radicalismo como partido político; su génesis y su doctrina* (Santiago: Editorial Universitaria, 1956), 44–45. Other sources do not mention this founding convention, probably because it was a rather informal affair.

72. León Echaiz, *Evolución*, 46. These names are also mentioned by León Echaiz, Espejo, and Koscina, and they appeared in the press of the period.

THE GIRONDINS OF CHILE

REMINISCENCES OF AN EYEWITNESS

(*The Last Supper of the French Girondins* by Monvoisin)

To Marcial González

THE GIRONDINS OF CHILE

The French Revolution of 1848 produced a powerful echo in Chile. For us poor colonials living on the shores of the Pacific Ocean, its predecessor in 1789, so celebrated in history, had been but a flash of light in our darkness. Half a century later, however, its twin had every mark of brilliant radiance. We had seen it coming, we studied it, we understood it, we admired it. We identified with its leaders, thanks to the lessons learned from them; with its events, thanks to the press; with its aspirations, thanks to our republic, which meant brotherhood across the seas and among peoples.

Thus it happened that the news of that sudden but profound change—the dethroning of a king, the fall of an arrogant and stubborn minister, the rise of men who through their books had been in a sense our teachers, the absolutely peaceful proclamation of a republic before the eyes of an astonished Europe, and the revitalizing shock that the collapse of that throne was producing one by one in all the rotten old monarchies of the Old World—in Germany, in Austria, in Prussia, even in Rome—this news produced general rejoicing in our country. High in the Vatican, Pius IX, whose residence in Chile had won him a kind of honorary citizenship in our hearts,[1] heralded reform; and in our timid land the aegis of his gleaming pontifical cape vindicated every bold step of that great change. The revolution in Europe was thus almost a Chilean revolution.

And Chile and Chilean society were ready for it. Though at the time there was no Chilean people—and there still is none[2]—we had our country's young, who were all we needed, an enlightened generation, hardworking, whose ideas rested on faith and whose deeds were impelled by high aspirations.[3] These were the heirs of Bello and Mora, of Gorbea and Sazié.

For its part, the government left the floodgates wide open for what was new in thought and action. There was a President in those days, and by his side there was a Cabinet. That President was Bulnes, and he had tamed the Araucanian Indians, pacified the Andes, and defeated the Bolivians. His ministers were, by turns, Montt or Vial, Varas or Sanfuentes, Pérez or Aldunate, Irarrázaval or Rengifo, Tocornal or García Reyes, men, all of them, whose thinking put them in the school of Bello or the school of Mora, and whose principles made them part of the democratic school of 1810.

In those days, as today, the Institute[4] was a seedbed of men; but the university was not yet a cemetery, nor was our national literature a corpse. On the contrary, our country's history was being born, its cradle illuminated by a radiant dawn. Lastarria, Benavente, the Amunáteguis, Father Salas, Santa María, Tocornal, Concha y Toro, Sanfuentes were gathering the scattered pages of a great age. The press already gave signs of its vigor, promising a robust life in the years to come. Espejo, Vallejos, Blanco Cuartín, Talavera, the three Mattas, Rafael Vial, Felipe Herrera, Eusebio Lillo, Ambrosio Montt, Francisco Marín and his illustrious sister, Pedro Gallo, Irisarri, Jacinto Chacón, Santiago Godoy, Santiago Lindsay, Víctor and Pío Varas, Francisco, Carlos, Juan, and Andrés Bello, Ramón Sotomayor, Francisco and Manuel Bilbao, the three Blests, Marcial González, Marcial Martínez, Diego Barros, José Antonio Torres, Paulino del Barrio, Juan Vicuña, Cristóbal Valdés, Salustio Cobo, the lamented Ruiz-Aldea, Santos Cavada, Ignacio Zenteno, Don Pedro Godoy, who was already a veteran of the pen and the sword, Isidoro Errázuriz, who was but a boy (but what a boy!), and hard on their heels, precocious but already imposing, the brothers Arteaga Alemparte, Vicente Reyes, inimitable in his effortless wit, Balmaceda, Eduardo de la Barra, brilliant in everything, Román Vial, and many others who flood into our memory (for memory is our only reference book), all of them historians, journalists, poets, critics, polemicists, most of them serious writers of a certain renown, each in his own field. And these in turn were followed by a mass of young men eager to learn, inclined to virtue, unruly at times, as in the Academy of Jurisprudence, but always filled with the love of justice and doggedly devoted to the task at hand.

Society as a whole felt itself spontaneously drawn to the powerful emotions of a life of innovations and new delights. For the first time, art unfolded its golden wings against our sapphire sky. Monvoisin had stretched his first canvases on the walls of his studio, and then Ciccarelli had brought us his rich southern palette.[5] Teresa Rossi was already singing like the sirens of whom we had heard in our cradles; and in our salons, graced then by the beauties that today shelter new flowers beneath their chaste shade, the splendid Pantanelli (Clorinda Corradi) revealed the secrets of heaven and its angels. All around you, you could feel movement, expansiveness, a powerful and brilliant vitality, as in those gay mornings of youth and summer when, with much domestic hustle and bustle, we set off on a pleasure trip. Where were we headed? No one asked. The beacon of the lighthouse gleamed on the horizon, and that was enough for each one of us to take his little boat and launch it boldly and confidently on the waves. Enthusiasm blew in the breeze, we heard the rustle of its wings on the shore, and each one of us shouted, "To sea, to sea!"

Today the shipwrecks of a quarter of a century litter the beach.

Yet let us for now continue our historian's task, going back to 1848 and setting out on the broad and foam-flecked sea of memories to recapture what we then witnessed.

The revolution that on February 24, 1848, had brought down the throne of Louis-Philippe had resulted less from the blind obstinacy of Guizot, his minister for nine years, than from the genius of a great poet, a simple deputy. Not one modern historian or critic fails to recognize the fact, elevated almost to dogma, that the publication of Lamartine's *Histoire des Girondins*, early in 1847, was the battering ram that set in motion and foreordained those days in February. "Reading that book," says Daniel Stern, "Europe felt the special shudder that precedes a hurricane."

By means of love and poetry, that work rehabilitated an age that until then had floated ghostlike in the popular mind amid the blood and flames of an incomprehensible catastrophe, the age of 1793, the age of the Terror. Lamartine brought light into that chaos. And he did more than that. With the incomparable magic of his style, unique in our century and perhaps in the centuries gone by, he surrounded each figure with a gleaming aura, no matter whether of love, of genius, of punishment, of glory, or of suffering. What his writer's and poet's spirit craved was to make each one of those men of 1789 and 1793, the most magnificent Girondins, parade before History, garbed as heroes and as martyrs, as demigods and as executioners, so that the memory of them and their very shadows might be engraved on the tablets of posterity. Even the guillotine was transformed in his hands, ceasing to be an implement of horror to become an instrument of study, of justice, and of glorification. That is why the illustrious Chateaubriand, defeated, depressed, and annoyed in the final hours of his life as an irreconcilable legitimist, said, "Monsieur de Lamartine has gilded the guillotine."

That is precisely why this immortal work was immensely popular in Chile, and especially in Santiago, more than any other book in the past or, probably, in the future. The first copy sold for six gold *onzas*,[6] the price of a whole library today; and the subsequent editions that came one after the other and in every language sold for similar amounts. In 1849 Lamartine confessed that in a single year the royalties from that book had brought him two and a half million francs, and the citizens of Chile contributed more than a few grains to form that mountain of gold whose peak was a sublime idea: the Republic!

Chileans are wont to become enthusiastic about whatever they buy, especially if they buy it dear, be it a book, a farm, an imported figure of a saint, a box in the theater, a government bond, or a stud stallion; yet quite apart from the power of fashion and habit, the *Histoire des Girondins* produced, by its very spirit and from its first appearance, an effect that no other fashion has exceeded in our country. In its way, this was more or less what was happening everywhere. In those days, everything was called *à la Girondine* or *à la Vergniaud* or *à la Barbaroux* or *à la Lamartine*, depending on individual preferences. In Paris, Alexandre Dumas and Auguste Maquet composed the "Chant des Girondins," which in 1870 served as a second "Marseillaise" of a once more republican France. "Mourir pour la patrie!"

Apart from all this, that revolutionary enthusiasm resounded in our hearts with a force all the greater because the book circulated among us at the same time as the news of the revolution that its spirit and its eloquence had brought about. The flash of lightning arrived here at the same moment as the clap of thunder, the life-giving breath of creation simultaneously with the appearance of the creature. The *Histoire des Girondins* thus came to be a prophetic book, like the Gospels, and in our eyes Lamartine shone with a blinding glory as though his figure were that of a divine herald. From 1848 to 1858, Lamartine was a demigod, like Moses. Pius IX, for some people, was God Himself, even before the proclamation of his infallibility.

We have already mentioned that the political, social, and literary atmosphere in which our people lived was inherently hospitable to the heat and energy coming from abroad. The February Revolution caught us during one of those periods when the chrysalis begins to move within the thick cocoon that enfolds us as a people, that is, during a political campaign.

The Vial cabinet had animated and fostered liberal sentiments in the country.[7] Following in the steps of Portales,[8] though in another direction, its chief had, early on, opened the gates of the public forum to the youth of the nation. And that generation, born of study and of the first skirmishes of journalism and debate, and stimulated by the recent reorganization of our schools, by the revitalization of our university —now old again and in decay—by the controversies about principles and goals successively launched by three highly impulsive literary, philosophical, and political publications— *El Siglo, El Crepúsculo,* and *El Progreso*—one of whose most daring innovations appeared in the famous trial and public triumph of Francisco Bilbao[9] in 1844—that generation, we were saying—enthusiastic, serious, at once brilliant, hardworking, and combative, one that simultaneously taught and learned—plunged into the electoral battle with noble fervor and saw its efforts crowned with an easy victory.

This is not the occasion to analyze how those congressional and municipal elections of March and April 1849 were conducted. They unquestionably took place on a grotesque stage, rather like all the comedies that our docile and patient Chilean people attend without realizing that they are the ones to pay the admission, the ones to perform onstage, and the ones to be booed when the curtain falls, and without taking into account the fact that those who boo them are the very ones who trample on their rights and honor. But not long ago we were recalling a glorious exception to those elections. The people of Valparaíso had, for the first time, triumphed over the invincible colossus that here we call the Authorities. It was David conquering Goliath!

::::

Be that as it may, the fact is that on June 1, 1849, for the first time in the parliamentary history of Chile, the doors of the Chamber of Deputies, the longtime fief of the deaf-mutes of every stripe of reaction, opened for a few independent spirits, for unfettered speech, for youthful and consequently exalted consciences. Tocornal, who had triumphed in Valparaíso, Lastarria, García Reyes, Juan Bello, Don Ignacio Víctor Eyzaguirre, Federico Errázuriz, Father Taforó, Marcial González, and Rafael Vial[10] took their seats that day in the midst of a public even more youthful and more enthusiastic than they, which gazed upon them with astonishment and undisguised sympathy. Much the same had happened with the new city council, which was a true political body when it was free, as it was in 1810, and a perpetual and servile conspiracy against the people when it was, as usual, submissive and docile. Now some of the youthful new deputies, like Errázuriz and González, joined it, and so, by direct election, did some resolute men like Pedro Ugarte, a spirit born for public life.

All this was taking place at the same time that men were most ardently reading the pages of the *Histoire des Girondins* and then the reports of the February Revolution and while the stack of dark clouds driven by the gales of revolution could be seen rising to the highest heavens. The book was therefore set aside in order to observe the action, and the image of the brave statesmen from beyond the seas came easily to be embodied in those familiar faces that symbolized such novel hopes and ideas. Not since 1810 had a city council been more popular in Santiago, even though the city had not chosen a single one of its members, the favorites among whom had, as always, bought their places, but paying not in gold but in ideas.

The battle therefore began early in the Chamber of Deputies; and on June 12, before parliament had been at work for a fortnight, the Vial-Sanfuentes cabinet, which had brought forth and shaped that assembly, was overthrown. It was followed by the transitional ministry of Pérez, Tocornal, and García Reyes.[11]

Were we attempting in these reminiscences, which are neither a political sketch nor a picture of the situation, but only what their title plainly states, *Reminiscences*—were we attempting here to trace the affinities among particular individuals and political aspirations, we might perhaps be justified in saying that the genuine Girondin element in the Chamber of 1849 was embodied in the Pérez ministry, and not in the spirit of agitation and love of novelty that was barred from power, for the former, besides being a moderating element, sought an intermediate solution to the crisis in General Aldunate's candidacy for the presidency of the republic. Seen in this light, Lastarria and the six or eight spirited youths sitting by his side were really in the position of Jacobins.

We are not, however, aiming to produce an analytical study of this sort, nor could we do so in a work like the one we now undertake. We are concerned only with certain comparisons between past and present, with certain useful or curious reminiscences, with certain evocations that may contain enduring lessons, or with those simple sensations of lawful pleasure that begin and end with every morning's reading of *El Ferrocarril*. It is a fashion of our time to decorate our gardens with coated glass balls that reproduce the surrounding landscape with admirable fidelity, their brittle convex surface taking in an entire countryside, with its mountains, flowers, sky, sunrise and sunset, and its light. Our undertaking is of this order. Beneath the shade of the trees of peace and silence we have hung the coated ball of our memory, allowing the reflections of the past and the present to strike its various prisms. Each one of these poor pages is one of those reflections, and nothing more.

And so we proceed.

From its first day, the triumphant cabinet donned its armor and launched such an attack against the benches of the majority that within a week the journalist Lastarria, the most brilliant and popular orator of his time, had occasion to test the strength of that majority,[12] which, however, stood by him for only a few hours (it was a majority patched together by higher authority, as are more or less all of them), as he led it to reject, by a vote of 31 to 11, a motion to table the reform of the press laws proposed by the minister Tocornal, even as his own motion for the plain and simple abrogation of that law passed by a vote of 37 to 5. We must add that in response to the same interests of the majority, the deputy Don Santos Lira had been elected president of the Chamber with 33 votes; and by a strange coincidence, 33 had been the majority with which Guizot, in December 1847, had opened the Chamber that was to overthrow him. That number has been fateful since the time of the Crucifixion, as the number 13 has been since the time of Judas. The Judases of 1849, however, were more than 13; by 1850 *the minority* had been completely crushed, though it remained free, frank, and fearless, with a newfound courage. It is to that minority that these brief notes of our memory are devoted, as is our enthusiasm, youthful then and youthful still.

After two years of constant struggle, the executive had finally managed completely to dominate the legislature. The government, with its solid power, had demonstrated that its law of gravity always trumps the laws of ascension that make up the dynamic of the spirit, that is, patriotism, justice, truth, virtue, duty, and responsibility before the people. This had occurred in such a manner and with such rapidity that all rifts had blended into one, a single dark and threatening background in the picture: a clash, that is, revolution, loomed on the horizon.

A logical consequence of this situation was that the parliamentary contingent of 1849, triumphant for a day and outcasts for two years, should carry on an open struggle against it. They had put forward a candidate for the presidency, so unexciting as to be soporific, but respectable and prestigious: the vice president of the Senate, Don Ramón Errázuriz, who at the time was sixty-five years old. An amazing phenomenon! The government of the old and powerful nominated the youngest president the country has ever had, one who had begun his public service as a school inspector;[13] the young men of the nascent party of progress had nominated an old man, a longtime proven conservative. Francisco Matta, a mercurial spirit but a sound and honorable soul, was the first to reproach the innovators of 1848 with this incongruity; but Matta forgot that a populist candidacy in Chile can never be spontaneous, because it always meets with a hostile reception. Every governmentally sponsored candidacy, no matter how prestigious, is necessarily a challenge, because it is by its very nature an insolent usurpation. As long, therefore, as the present system remains in force and grows ever more abusive, every nomination of candidates is bound to be a duel to the death, to the detriment and dishonor of the republic.

This did not make the campaign any less violent, less tinged by hatreds and buffeted by storms. The conservative candidacy had from its very beginning been an implacable challenge. Ever since the first parliamentary sessions of 1849, a presentiment had graven in every breast the accursed word *Loncomilla!*[14] Why? We have already said why: because the country was in the grip of passion, and every spontaneous candidacy arising from it had of necessity to be one of struggle against the candidacy that represented the power and victory of the government.

And this is the point at which we truly begin our story, which up to this point we have cloaked beneath the apparently undecipherable name *The Girondins of Chile.*

A few days ago, a good many people were greatly startled to learn that we have had a Robespierre in Chile, and now the fact is known to everyone. Well, in like manner we shall now justify our title by means of reminiscences as simple and almost homey as they are true, concerning things that took place but yesterday and that may therefore be recalled by many whose hair still retains its original color. Ours already bears witness to many a winter, but we shall try to prove that with its color our head has not lost its memory.

It was the month of October of the year 1850. The chambers had just concluded their sessions after the most violent debates, of which a pale reflection remains in the official records and press of that time. Intense agitation seethed in every spirit, voracious like the flames of its anger. During the dreadful night of August 19, 1850, there had been an attempt to quell the ardor of those parliamentary and journalistic debates by using cudgels to impose silence on the Sociedad de la Igualdad, or Egalitarian Society,[15] but that bloody scene had only inflamed the temper of the public to the utmost. Within a few hours after the attack, the club's quarters had grown too small for the crowd, and the meetings were moved to an unfinished but spacious theater on the Calle de Duarte.[16]

Every Thursday and Sunday this place held from four to six thousand persons, whom Francisco Bilbao electrified with majestic speeches. Bilbao, a simple writer with a biblical style who sometimes, like Lacunza,[17] was almost unintelligible, was also a great orator, the leading popular orator of his time, just as Lastarria was leader of the troops in parliament. The club had become an army, and the army was a threat; and if Santiago, whose people are numerous but lack and have always lacked a soul, had felt a single spark fall into its vital center, which was that famous club, the shouts of its leaders would have swept away the government on one of those placid spring afternoons of October, with the coming and going of one of those processions that filled the Alameda before or after the sessions of parliament. All of that, however, was only harmless sound and fury, because Bilbao led the march like a visionary, carrying a liberty tree made of . . . glass beads! A most appropriate battle standard for his followers! In the Convention of 1793, Barrère, as he voted for the execution of Louis XVI, had said, "The tree of liberty can only be irrigated with blood." That Chilean tree of liberty in 1850 had been irrigated only with leftover water from the morning *mate* of the Poor Clares, whose convent was a prolific producer of that sort of trinket.

There was, however, constant talk everywhere about the state of siege that would necessarily result from what in Chile has been called the legitimate expression of public opinion. Then as now, and for all the tergiversations and artful mystifications of our legislators, a declaration of a state of siege depended exclusively on the will, or rather, the omnipotence of the president. But General Bulnes, who had the makings of a great statesman, held off, and that's the explanation for the delay. Had President Bulnes wanted it, time would have rushed forward, and the battle of Loncomilla would have taken place a year or two before it actually did, because there is something that no omnipotence can derail, and that something is the preordained course of human events. A dictator can play with the hands of the clock, like a child; but the hour will strike unless he smashes the whole mechanism with his bullets. And even then, the fleeting hour will find a place to strike, and its echo will gather those who are ever awaiting the sign.

With this constant threat hanging over them, the city's deputies, the writers and orators, and the plain egalitarians of 1849 met frequently, by day in the printing plant of *El Progreso,* which at that time was located in the historic building on the Calle de Huérfanos[18] then numbered 32 and replaced, after its demolition, by the center of the MacClure Gate, and by night in the house of the mother of the ex-minister Vial, which has now been rebuilt and is No. 64 on the same street, between Morandé and Teatinos.

Almost all the leaders of the Liberal Party, then dubbed the Egalitarian Party, attended these meetings. Pedro Ugarte, who as a judge had presided over the trial of the cudgelers of August 19; Lastarria, the party's leader in parliament; José Miguel Carrera, who was to be one of its military chiefs; the two Bilbaos, Francisco and Manuel, its public champions; Eusebio Lillo, its poet; Santa María, who inspired it; Federico Errázuriz, who counseled it; Francisco Marín, who represented its honesty; Manuel Recabarren, who stood for its firmness; Juan Bello, who embodied its distinction; and last, among others of less consequence, like the author of these reminiscences, Santiago Arcos, whose aim was to be the tutelary spirit of that patriotic club, pushing it, less through design or secret intention than by the force of his vivid imagination, toward a dark cloak and dagger sort of rebellion, "Spanish style."

These daily meetings took place in one of the courtyard rooms next to the street, on the right hand as you went in; and they used to last from late afternoon, when people came back from the Tajamar, the Alameda, or the Puente de Palo, very popular places at that time for a cool summer walk, until after midnight. No one was in charge; no one tried to run things. It was a democratic organization, so much so that the only acknowledged leader it could produce was a veteran of the War of Independence, a relative of the Vial family, who since 1811 was called Pistolita in honor of the pistol shot he had fired on Santiago's main square on the day of Figueroa's attempt at a royalist coup.[19] His real name, like that of his father, was Juan de Dios Vial, and he worked as a border guard in the Andes, which made him well qualified to look after a political club that was always like a volcano on the verge of an eruption. That worthy old man therefore kept the keys of the club and at night closed the mansion's heavy door after the last member had left.

In that locale news was disseminated, plans were discussed, emissaries were sent, and articles were written for the press, speeches for other clubs, and proclamations for the people. Everyone was convinced that a coup d'état was imminent, and no one could or wanted to stay out of it. It is a fact that in those days men looked on a prison cell with the same *sangfroid* as today they do a judge's bench, and exile to the remote south seemed quite as acceptable as a seat in parliament. Politics disciplines men of mettle as war disciplines the soldier. After six months in the field, there are no more raw recruits or deserters or spies or marauders; the rabble has remained in the rear guard, and only calm heads and proud breasts are to be seen in the first ranks.

Because of the similarity between two historical moments, one of the favorite topics of conversation during those daily meetings arose from the likewise daily reading of Lamartine's *Girondins,* with its accounts of the deeds of those celebrated men, their eloquence, their patriotism, their mistakes, their sublime and lamentable sacrifice, the posthumous glory that radiated from their genius and from their bloody end. And that was when the figures and names of each one of those Girondins of Chile began to appear on the covert stage of the nascent revolution, their personalities and schools of thought preserved intact in our secret annals.

Analogy, assimilation, sympathies, presentiment, or simple whim had led each member of the club to choose his revolutionary nom de guerre or to accept it from his companions; and as so often happens, these colorful cloaks for a situation as serious as had been its foreign predecessor were not devoid of wit and character. We Chileans are by nature imitators, especially when imitation costs us nothing; and those revolutionary baptisms were performed free of charge every evening, and even with tea and cake thrown in.

Thus Lastarria had justly been given exclusive rights to the name of Brissot, the propagandist and leader of the Gironde, whose political ideas had epitomized his whole party and whose skill in combat had earned him the commanding role.

Just as appropriately, Francisco Bilbao became known only by the name of Vergniaud, the most illustrious orator of the

Gironde, to whom Mirabeau, when he died in the flower of his youth, at forty-two, at the very outset of the Revolution, seemed to have bequeathed the arena so that he might brandish his words and his glory.

Manuel Recabarren, Bilbao's close friend at the time, had taken the name of that brave and handsome son of Marseilles, Barbaroux, who had fought at the Tuileries, gun in hand, to dethrone a king, just as Recabarren later fought at the artillery barracks, composed and valiant like his forerunner.

After Brissot and Vergniaud, two of the most notable among the Girondins properly speaking, that is, among the deputies of Bordeaux and its department, were Ducos and Boyer-Fonfrède, brothers-in-law, whom Monvoisin shows in his painting *The Last Supper of the Girondins* exchanging a final close embrace in homage to life, home, and patriotism. They were brave young sons of Bordeaux, full of life, joie de vivre, and enthusiasm, only twenty-eight and twenty-six years old, respectively. That was about the age of Juan Bello and Rafael Vial, close companions since their earliest school days and especially since the time of those classes that Bello's father had held in his home for the most distinguished of the young students. Rafael Vial became Boyer-Fonfrède and Juan Bello, Ducos; but due to his fervor and sparkle, Bello also received the name of the first tribune of the French Revolution, Camille Desmoulins, even though the latter had not been a comrade of the Girondins but, on the contrary, their involuntary executioner.

Domingo Santa María brilliantly bore the name of Louvet, the impetuous orator and popular poet of the Gironde; and, finally, the title of Mayor Pétion fell on Marcial Gómez,

who since 1849 had had a superb record as a man of principles and political honesty in his double role of alderman and
deputy.

Let no one, however, think that the roster of Chile's
Girondins was limited to the list of deputies, orators, and
martyrs of the French party. Lamartine's work had popular-
ized all the outstanding men and great characters of the Revolution of '89, to the point that the generous spirit of his
book has appropriately been termed by a modern critic, Pas-
cal Duprat, "the posthumous reconciliation between Vergniaud and Robespierre." Imbued with the same even-handed
veneration, the members of the club that met on the Calle de
Huérfanos took their noms de guerre as they pleased,
whether from among the Jacobins or from the Gironde or
even from other intermediate revolutionary groups. Thus the
Amunáteguis, for example, honest men but cautious, had
leapt over the benches of the stormy Convention of 1793 and
had cheerfully adopted the names and noble fellowship of
those three illustrious brothers who had represented moder-
ation and sensible patriotism in the Constituent Assembly,
the three Lameths who, though born in different years—
1756, 1757, and 1760—functioned as triplets. Miguel Luis
Amunátegui became Théodore Lameth, and Gregorio Víctor, Charles Lameth. Manuel Amunátegui—the third
Lameth, Alexandre—still remained in the antechamber
awaiting his brothers' order to join them.

The three French Lameths, by the way, had led remark-
ably homogeneous lives, for all had fought with Lafayette in
the War of Independence of the United States. As educated
men, all three, thanks to their travels and military campaigns,

had a perfect knowledge not only of their native language but also of English. Later, during the time of the Terror, for which their souls had not been formed, they emigrated to Germany, whose language they also learned, which perhaps brought them no great benefit, for though it is true that Charles V used to say that "a man is as many men as he knows languages," those austere republicans no doubt believed that two languages are more than enough, because no matter how many a schoolboy might know he remains a schoolboy, while Charles V was king and emperor and whatever else he chose.

Just as the two Amunáteguis, moderate, peaceful, studious, timid perhaps but responsible, faithful in their attendance at every evening meeting, had received names that evoked a social comportment more than a political stance, so the godfathers of the egalitarian club of the Vial-Formas mansion discreetly reserved ecclesiastical titles for the two priests who had come to join that liberal gathering, which now is hermetically closed to tonsure and miter in the name of today's extravagant notion of liberty. There were nineteen priests in the Convention of 1793; but the agitators of Santiago, all of whom, with the exception of Francisco Bilbao and Santiago Arcos, were sincere Catholics, pronounced the name of Vice President Eyzaguirre[20] only in association with that of the Abbé Sieyès, the famous vicar of Chartres, and the name of the deputy Taforó only in association with that of the philanthropical Bishop Grégoire, another member of the Convention. Was this assignment of a miter prophetic?

Pedro Ugarte, who was not only no freethinker but a devout believer and rigid ascetic, had received the name of

Danton; and to be sure, saving the matter of religion there was no better epithet for that energetic, impetuous, and resourceful character. Likewise the name of Saint-Just was bestowed on Manuel Bilbao, on account of his remarkable resemblance to the handsome French triumvir, whose blue eyes and long hair and mien he bore, almost like a portrait. Eusebio Lillo, close companion of the younger Bilbao, as Manuel Recabarren was of his brother Francisco, gloriously bore the name of Rouget de Lisle, the inspiring author of "La Marseillaise," because like him he was both a soldier and a poet.

Since we are writing these pages in the countryside, unable to consult either notes or other witnesses, our memory is not entirely clear concerning the mythological appellations of some other personages of our revolutionary era, such as Federico Errázuriz, Manuel Guerrero, José Miguel Carrera, and the Argentine general Don Bartolomé Mitre, who at the time was a simple journalist and later became president of the Argentine Confederation,[21] and who used to come from Valparaíso to take part in those discussions that created a community of souls, forerunner of the community of dungeons where we were to meet not long after.

Yet although these reflections of youthful memory have dimmed in the mirror of the years, we recall quite vividly which of our friends were chosen to bear in our revolutionary gatherings the names then most abhorred of the time of the Terror.

What we are about to recount will seem incredible today; but it is nonetheless true that the heir of Maximilien Robespierre was Francisco Marín, the purest and most benevolent among those souls, even though in his speeches he would pronounce terrifying judgments on the lives, fortunes, and even wives and daughters of his adversaries. Those punishments, however, lasted as long as does the foam that crowns the breaking azure wave, for the tranquility of goodness and reason immediately reasserted its complete dominion over that eminently virtuous character, which, to be happy and harmonious, lacked only that gift, sweet and terrible but by the same token the indispensable element of balance in the lives of all animate creatures, that God found lacking in Adam when He saw him wandering alone and wrathful through the forests of Eden.

As for Marat, his name was bestowed, or capriciously chosen by its recipient, with a much greater appearance of justification. Santiago Arcos bore his pseudonym cheerfully and maintained that whoever had given it to him had acted very sensibly, for though he had been born in Santiago's episcopal palace, on the Calle de Huérfanos and next door to the political club where all this was happening, he never spoke of the Chilean revolution but as would a Parisian Jacobin or an Italian *carbonari*. Poor Santiago Arcos! He took a strange pride in wickedness, and at bottom he was good, compassionate, humane, and even philanthropic in his way. "Make use of your dagger, my boy," he wrote from exile in California to one of his confidants in Santiago, "and let the regeneration of Chile be written on the hides of the tories!" These were his very words; yet the only genuine part of that language is its picturesqueness, because its ferocity was false, and he himself knew it would be understood that way. Twenty years later, in 1871, I met him again in Naples, old, tired of adventures, rich, conservative, full of aches and pains, and, indeed, a tory in everything except his view of death. His nom de guerre turned out to have been prophetic in this, because he expired in a bath of the River Seine like Marat, who, thanks perhaps to a whim, had once become his model.

For a moment Santiago Arcos had a rival for his terrible name. This occurred the night of August 19, when a pale and bloodied Rafael Vial was carried to his house on the Calle de Huérfanos on the shoulders of the egalitarians, his head swathed in bandages after a cowardly attack by the henchmen of Isidro Jara, alias "The Swineherd." His injuries were not serious, but during those days, as his friends stood around the wounded man's bed, the naturally dramatic appearance of the victim and the outrageousness of the attack called up memories of the dagger of Charlotte Corday. Things fortunately did not turn out that way for Rafael, whom the sharp wit of Vallejos had by then begun to transform into the Raphaël of Lamartine.[22] Rafael Vial would have been inconsolable had he died at the hands of Isidro Jara, swineherd and captain of street toughs. Now dying by a woman's dagger, that would have been a different story!

But if the sickbed of the "martyr deputy" (as they called him) and group leader among the egalitarians lacked the heroic presence of Charlotte, did the Girondins of Santiago have a Jeanne Roland like the one who supplied the Parisian Girondins with shelter, passion, and heroism until she perished by their side? Who knows? In Monvoisin's painting, which we shall comment on presently, a veiled woman appears, her stance and countenance raising the spirits of those who are to die with and perhaps for her. The veil is thick, yet the eye whose retina retains the image of Santiago's renowned beauties of that time can still discern that that woman is no foreign image but the likeness of a well-known and noble matron of those days. Without revealing the mysteries of art or offending the truth of history, we can avouch that this is a Chilean Madame Roland.

These are the portraits of the outstanding members of those political clubs in Santiago in 1850 and 1851, who brought about the days, as dreadful as they were inevitable, that history now mournfully recalls under the rubrics "April 20" and "Loncomilla," the first and last act of the bloodiest drama of our political existence.[23] Those leaders, like those of another time and place whom they had taken as their models, undoubtedly had many a weakness and, like their models, committed the great blunder of beheading themselves, for just as the vote of Vergniaud and his colleagues for the death sentence against Louis XVI was a form of suicide, because it was a vote of egoism against conscience, so the abandonment of the candidacy of the civilian patriot Errázuriz in favor of that of General Cruz,[24] a dyed-in-the-wool champion of the old conservative cause, was political suicide for that two-year-old party, more an inevitable flaw of the situation in which they found themselves than a crime of political judgment, but one whose results were soon evident.

Even had they triumphed with Cruz on the banks of the Maule,[25] the Santiago Girondins, after their hymns and palms of victory, would have succumbed in the streets of their own capital, for in the 1851 campaign General Cruz showed admiration, sympathy, and true and profound respect only for the two men who were the closest advisers of his successful rival, García Reyes and Tocornal, the former being General Bulnes's secretary-general and the latter, his adjutant general. Cruz's first cabinet would perhaps have been chosen from among the tumultuous deputies of 1849, but the subsequent and permanent one would have been selected from the camp of the vanquished. Such is the inexorable course of history and of human logic, a simple text ever open before those who govern but deciphered only by those who look upon it from below, because the others close their eyes so as not to read it until they have once more sunk down.

"The Pontius Pilates of kingship," Lamartine called his heroes for the act of political cowardice that cleared their own way to the scaffold, and the poet spoke with all the fairness of Tacitus. An equally severe judgment could not, however, be pronounced on their Chilean imitators, nor could one apply to them the words that harsh Proudhon dared to write about their models, words we dare not repeat because of their brutal forcefulness. Far from it. When, after the hour of merry talk, the hour of stern duty struck, each one of them showed that he knew how to honor his obligations; and the most interesting part of this comparison, which is not always appropriate, is that in the time of their persecution these men were loyal to each other. Their fallings out, their jealousies, and their rivalries began only when they prospered and came to power, a failing inherent in human weakness that causes Michelet, in judging the Girondins of '93 and envisaging the possibility of their triumph on the very day of their fall, to exclaim, "Et moi, j'aurais aussi voté contre eux!"

Another point of similarity that favored the bestowal of old revolutionary names to our homegrown apprentice revolutionaries was the fact that all sprang from the same point of origin: first of all the courts of law, then the political club, and finally the halls of parliament. Lastarria, Errázuriz, Santa María, Marcial González, and Francisco Marín had been lawyers, like the Girondins of Bordeaux, and like them had gone on to be agitators and members of a legislative assembly.

Equally worthy of the kind of explanation that comes effortlessly to our pen without checking its speed or its spontaneity is the sum of the days allotted to the real Girondins in their fleeting and hence glorious lives. Their biographers and historians have, in effect, noted that of the twenty-one who mounted the scaffold on October 30, 1793, half had not reached the age of twenty-six, and only one had lived more than forty years. Vergniaud and Pétion were only thirty-four at the time of their fall, for both had been born in 1759, the former in Limoges, the latter in Chartres; Louvet was younger by a year; Brissot was twenty-nine; and Barbaroux, like Saint-Just, had barely reached the age of twenty-six when he took his own life in 1794.

The men whom their fate cast as Girondins among us were not granted more years than these. In 1851 Lastarria's age was exactly the same as that of Pétion and Vergniaud, and his name, like that of the latter, was Victorino; Santa María was approaching the age of his revolutionary pseudonym, Louvet; and Francisco Bilbao and Manuel Recabarren could match their age and their striking handsomeness against those of Barbaroux. In 1851 Pedro Ugarte had reached the precise age of Danton on the scaffold, thirty-five years; and—a persistent warning of fate and foreboding!—from then on he always said, when among friends, that he would die as soon as he had reached the half-century mark. This he foretold us in Lima in 1860, repeating it to us in the same city, where he had taken up residence, in 1865 and again in 1866. When the time came he returned to die, as he had announced three times while in exile, in Santiago, the city he had most loved and, in his moments of melancholy or bitterness, most profoundly despised; and he did so after completing precisely fifty years of a stormy and manly life. We say this because there were two entirely different men in Pedro Ugarte: the irascible man and the great-hearted man. His end was in keeping with this nature.

When Georges Danton's friends advised him to leave France and save himself from the scaffold that Robespierre was preparing for him, he steadfastly refused and exclaimed, "Why should I flee? Is it on the soles of our shoes that we bear the dust of our fatherland?" And that is why Pedro Ugarte, thrice exiled from Chile in the space of fifteen years, always came home, and that is why the dust of his bones will rest mingled forever with the dust of the land that gave him birth.

The senior member of that group was Francisco Marín, who in 1851 was nearing forty and, like Palazuelos, was still a dashing bachelor. Thus when he received the pseudonym of Robespierre, which he still bears among his most devoted friends, his age already exceeded that of the celebrated Jacobin when he mounted the scaffold. And so we can assure the incredulous, for their edification, that in Chile, instead of one Robespierre, we have had two, one of whom is still alive.[26]

For all that, the fictions of every period, like its facts, are bound to come to a resolution, and a denouement, serious and even threatening for the revolutionary leaders of the rejuvenated Liberal Party, did loom in 1851.

That hour tolled precisely in the days we have chosen for presenting these reminiscences, because on November 7, 1850,[27] a general commotion broke out whose inevitable result was the long-anticipated declaration of a state of siege, which brought about a political disaster more serious than that transient rage and panic. That disaster was the conversion of the as yet undecided General Bulnes to wholehearted support of the candidacy of Montt, who from then on came to be called "the law and order candidate."

That insurrection by a high-minded but unthinking populace led to the first dispersion of the Girondins of Santiago, and immediately thereafter, April 20 consummated their undoing and led to their total disappearance from the political scene. These developments paralleled the fate of the French Girondins in that, like the latter after their banishment in June 1793, our Girondins withdrew into the interior of the provinces to spread the fire of their patriotism and their despair in all directions. It seems to us that we can still hear the fervent, enthusiastic, and mesmerizing voice of Juan Bello on the night before the terrible battle in April, as he invited his comrades in the Girondin club of the Calle de Huérfanos to take refuge, if only to forge new swords, in the provinces of Aconcagua, Valparaíso, and Colchagua, in case, as was then expected at any minute, the government should outstrip the people with a definitive coup d'état. On that night of the last meager feast of the last parliamentary session, others spoke of going to Copiapó, to Concepción, or to the border, which was guarded by mounted troops and by the Carampangue Regiment.

There was something dreadful in the air at that time. A strong earthquake on April 2 was the forerunner and tocsin. April 20 was, in fact, nothing but the bloody clash of two adversaries who had been stalking each other day and night and sleeping for the previous six months with their pistols under their pillows. That is why both fought to the death and without seconds.

These scenes, memories, and tragedies, however, belong to another page of these reminiscences of yesterday, of which only an old man can speak as a witness; and so we put an end to this episode with the scattering of that band that bore fictitious names, to be sure, but that in character and circumstances was closely linked to the political party immortalized by the genius of a poet. At least all that we relate of our Girondins is not invented but factual and vouched for by our personal observation; and though it is true that our picture lacks the somber tones of poignant scaffold and dazzling glory, those spirited imitators of a noble revolutionary tradition did not for all that fail to take their proper place and fully live up to its demands, according to the mission and resolve that was the lot of each one of them.

In this way Lastarria, Marcial González, Federico Errázuriz, Santiago Arcos, and others were banished to Peru in November 1850,[28] only to be included in the harsher and far more extensive banishment of 1851. Juan Bello forced the police to seize him atop the grave of Colonel Urriola, glorifying the vanquished on the day after he perished on the streets of Santiago; and despite the government's profound respect for his illustrious father and of the tears of his young wife, an exemplar of beauty and feminine graces, he was deported together with Mitre, like him a noble and almost voluntary prisoner. "Camille Desmoulins" had found his "Lucile."

Confined in a ship loaded with foul-smelling guano, Pedro Ugarte, the heart and soul of the exiguous civilian component of the largely military uprising of April 20, was sent to an Irish port; yet this punishment, excessively long for a man of his physical constitution and moral temper, was no match for his proud integrity.

Francisco Bilbao, Manuel Recabarren, Domingo Santa María, Rafael Vial, and many others sought constantly to carry on the struggle while in hiding in the capital. The Amunáteguis honorably forfeited the posts that were the source of their daily bread; and Eusebio Lillo, soldier and poet, went off to enlist in the heroic battalions of armed citizens that fought for a doomed cause on the field of Reyes, on the far bank of the Maule. And—a historical rarity, but normal among us—only the man who had inherited the most dreaded name of the French Revolution, Robespierre, remained quietly at home, lamenting the misfortunes of his fatherland in eloquent pamphlets that for the time being were but the extinguished torches of liberty. Santiago Arcos emigrated to California, then to Mendoza in Argentina, then to the River Plate, then to Paraguay, where he served as a soldier, and, finally, to Paris, where he resumed his career as a banker, like his father, who in Chile had created the market in government debt and the practice of carrying on not the business of the state but business with and against the state. That fashion has, since 1820, lasted for more than half a century, but does it not seem that it will come to an end in our days?

In the meantime, the wave of fascination that our century's most polished (we shall not say most accurate) account of the Revolution set off in the Chilean public was not confined, here or in France or in the whole of Europe, to the field of politics; and just as in Paris the pages of *Les Girondins* spawned dramas as well as barricades, music as well as immortal song ("Le Chant du départ"), so in Santiago an artist of the great revolutionary school of painting laid hold of one of its most moving anecdotes and reproduced it. This is the origin of the famous canvas by Monvoisin,[29] which our title has forced us to treat as a secondary part of this study, unlike what we did in our comment on *The Fall of Robespierre.*

The picture is at any rate suitable only for a superficial and desultory analysis, because the illustrious artist, weighed down by age, gave free rein to his own imagining, which simply reproduced a written inspiration and consequently lacked previous study, precise setting, animating philosophy, characters, movement, color—in a word, life. *The Last Supper of the Girondins* contains five or six admirable figures fully worthy of the painter of *The 9 Thermidor,* among them that of Vergniaud contemplating his final hour on his watch, the fraternal embrace of Ducos and Boyer-Fonfrède, the untidy but expressive and distinctive figure of Brissot, a cloth around his head in the manner still favored by men who spend a sleepless night before their execution, and, finally, the haughty and aristocratic head of Gensonné, agitated by wrath and pride as he hears his name in the list of the condemned that the warden of the prison is reading at that moment.

Apart from this, however, and from the draftsmanship, which is generally correct for the group of Girondins, though not for the crowd of guards and populace that is rushing against the door, the painting loses the great charm of a work of art, because it is a painting that lacks truth.

Painted in Chile in 1852–54,[30] *The Girondins* consequently does not contain a single portrait and is merely the rendering of two pages by Lamartine on one larger page of canvas. The painting is colossal and for that very reason inferior to that of Robespierre, in which everything is concentrated, throbbing with life, and speaking to the viewer. The *Robespierre* is a tumultuous scene, a tempest in the life of a naturally tempestuous people, based on history and copied from nature. *The Girondins* is only an allegory that reproduces another allegory, which explains its slight effect on the retina and soul of the viewer.

There are in fact those who doubt that the last supper of the Girondins was an episode in the story of their real death and not a poetic fable spun by the muse as part of a written epic. Riouffe, a member of the Convention who was held in the same prison as the Girondins and was in daily communication with them, says only that they spent that night singing patriotic songs until the coming of dawn, but says nothing about the feast, the toasts, the flaming punch that cast purplish and blue reflections onto the faces of the group. He makes not the slightest mention of this, yet in his *Mémoires d'un détenu* he recounts far more trivial incidents and details about the farewells and the executions of his fellow-prisoners in the Conciergerie.

Lamartine himself, who as a poet does not shy from taking liberties, cites, in his book devoid of notes and references ("so as not to clutter the text"), no witness in support of his creation other than the Abbé Lambert, whom, however, no writer of the time mentions; and even of the account of that witness, the poet-historian merely affirms that a great many of his details are "véridiques comme la conscience et fidèles comme la mémoire d'un dernier ami," which, when you come down to it, does not vouch for a single truth, because how many false consciences are there among men for every "truthful conscience," and how many memories of last friends, including those of executors, have been *unfaithful*, especially once the "last friend" is no longer among the living!

Even if the essence of that fantastic midnight drama is authentic, the painter has taken all the liberties his brush needed to arrange his inverisimilar scene, on top of the countless liberties already taken by the poet with his details. Thus the appearance of Madame Roland at the final banquet of the Girondins is an absolute anachronism, because on the night of October 29, 1793, that superior and pure woman, who inspired and befriended the Girondins but was not their comrade, was not in the Conciergerie but in the Abbaye, a far-distant prison. Madame Roland was taken to the Conciergerie only after the execution of the Girondins, and she mounted the scaffold ten days after they did, on November 9, 1793.

Furthermore, it is well known that the guillotine was at that time permanently located on the Place de la Révolution (now called Place de la Concorde, even though the discord among the French grows sharper day by day); yet in order to consolidate the acts of the drama, the painter shows the frame and blade of that horrible machine next to the window on the left where the first light of dawn is beginning to seep in—another falsification of history, because their executioners did not enter the dungeon of the Girondins until ten in the morning, and they were guillotined at one o'clock in the midst of a pouring rain. And the livid corpse of Valazé, lying on a stretcher on the floor while his friends and colleagues raise their glasses to their immortal souls and the brotherhood of the tomb: Is this a felicitous and harmonious detail or an excessively theatrical contrast?

It is true that Monvoisin merely picked up with the tip of his fertile brush the wealth of personal details produced by the even more fertile imagination of the great modern poet; and it is likewise true that the latter felt supremely free to enter into the affairs, situations, physiognomies, and even the innermost thoughts and emotions of his heroes. In truth, Lamartine speaks of the banquet of the Girondins as though he had been one of the guests: he sings and weeps with them and raises his glass for their toasts. Word for word he reproduces the sublime farewells and the majestic consolations that Vergniaud directed at his companions; he repeats the witty outbursts of Ducos as though he were hearing them; he listens to the quiet dialogues between Brissot and Lasource; and his innocent indiscretion even seems to have taken note of each sin that the Abbé Fauchet was confessing in his cell to the Abbé Émery. So detailed is his account of each and every one!

Yet the poet goes farther still, because his searching glance penetrates each one of those impassible foreheads, enters into the deepest recesses of those heroic hearts, and surmises, feels, and tells what each of them is thinking or suffering. Thus the Girondin Carra, a man of mature years who had written some books about Wallachia and Moldavia, was, to hear the historian tell it, reconstructing the map of Europe in his mind and in his cell; the Abbé Fauchet was beating his breast as a sign of deepest repentance; Brissot was thinking of God; Sillery was thinking of the duc d'Orléans; and finally Lasource, unable to do anything else, "was illuminating (I quote word for word from the book) the depths of anarchy with the fires of his ardent imagination."[31] And this charming spinner of tales, who recounts the cruelties of history with the exquisite grace of poetic fable, does not stop even here, for with his own hands he wraps each victim of the Terror in the shroud of his glory, helps the executioners in their final task of preparing his neck for the fatal blade, and when all is over neatly installs each one in his coffin.

In our childhood we have seen the same cleverness, or even greater, displayed by a coffin manufacturer, who was neither poet nor historian, but who on the wall opposite his shop had noted the height of all the leading inhabitants of the city, drawing a pencil line at head level as they passed by, with a mark to distinguish between the sexes. In that way, when pale Death came to knock at the palace gates of the mighty, that tireless entomber of the living was never caught by surprise, and each customer was taken care of more or less to measure, as in the Casa Francesa or some other elegant tailor's shop.

In this way genius embellishes and poeticizes the most ordinary discoveries; and Lamartine, as he measured each Girondin to construct the pedestal of his fame in keeping with his stature, was, without knowing it, plagiarizing the farsighted cabinet maker of Santiago.

No, Lamartine's work is no history. It is a legend, a song, an epic, and hence its universal luster, because what is most widespread in the human race is its profound credulity and, at the same time, its magnanimous deference to the greatness of superior souls. That is why the Ancients invented the Titans and the gods. "Monsieur de Lamartine's book," one of his critics (Larousse, 1874) has rightly said, "is the most unorthodox of all histories, but at the same time the most interesting of all poems."

Here, though we fall short of our aim, we put an end to our task. Like the Girondins before the fall of monarchy, we live in days of total uncertainty and terrible problems.

Yet let us not lose hope! As for us, simple workmen now as before, we take up the humble cloak of the pilgrim of old, hung away for five years on the wall of wearisome obligations. In our recovered tranquility, we rejoin the ordinary life of working men and therefore sign with a name that at that very time was not wholly disdained by our compatriots.

SAN-VAL
Santiago, October 1876

Notes

1. Giovanni Maria Mastai, the future Pius IX, visited Chile in 1824 as part of a mission (the Muzi mission) that sought to improve the relations between church and state, which had been strained since the time of the struggle for independence. As pope, he initially supported the European revolutions of 1848. (Editor's note, as are all others not otherwise identified)

2. The author is referring to the general lack of participation in public and political affairs by the masses or lower classes.

3. The reference is to the liberal young men of the ruling class.

4. The Instituto Nacional was a state-sponsored secondary school.

5. Monvoisin and Ciccarelli were European painters who lived in Chile and acquired followers among native artists.

6. The *onza* was a gold coin worth about sixteen U.S. dollars during the nineteenth century. (Translator's note)

7. Manuel Camilo Vial Formas was President Bulnes' last minister of the interior. Although officially a member of the Conservative (*pelucón*) Party, he had liberal propensities.

8. Diego José Portales was a Conservative minister in the 1830s and de facto head of the government. He created the conservative and authoritarian system that ruled Chile until 1871.

9. Francisco Bilbao was a passionate young liberal and ardent admirer of revolutionary France.

10. All the foregoing were young liberals.

11. Pérez, Tocornal, and García Reyes were all conservative politicians.

12. A majority which, in 1850, became a minority.

13. The reference is to Manuel Montt, an ultraconservative born in 1809, president from 1851 to 1861.

14. The Battle of Loncomilla (December 18, 1851) confirmed the presidency of Manuel Montt and for the time being eliminated the last traces of the "Girondins of Chile" and the "Spirit of '48."

15. The Egalitarian Society was founded in March 1850 by young liberals, many of them "Chilean Girondins." It quickly gained strong support among the liberal oligarchy and elements of the lower classes. It aimed to carry out radical social and political reforms, following the example of the first months of the French revolution of 1848.

16. Before August 19, the Egalitarian Society used to meet in the rooms and offices of the Philharmonic Society, which have now been converted into storehouses and stables for the house of Mr. Rafael Larraín on the Calle de las Monjitas. After the events of August 19, several thousand new members joined the Society; and among these one of the first was Don Ramón Errázuriz, who from that point on was the Liberal Party's candidate for the presidency. To accommodate the crowd, the club moved to a vast theater, still under construction, on the Calle Duarte, where later the Casas de Avendaño were built. If memory serves, that property belonged at the time to the councilman Don Luis Ovalle, an important member of the Liberal Party. (Author's note)

17. Manuel Lacunza, born in Chile in 1731, was a Jesuit priest and celebrated millenarian theologian. After the expulsion of the Jesuits in 1767, he lived in Italy until his death in 1801. His work *La venida del Mesías en gloria y majestad* (The coming of the Messiah in glory and majesty) was world-renowned.

18. Calle de Huérfanos is a street in the very center of Santiago.

19. Lieutenant Colonel Tomás de Figueroa, a royalist, organized a coup against the newly established nationalist government on April 1, 1811. Upon its failure, he was executed.

20. Eyzaguirre was vice president of the Chamber of Deputies.

21. At the time of which the author writes, Mitre was in exile in Chile.

22. "The Raphaël of Lamartine" alludes to *Raphaël*, a prose narrative by Lamartine (1849). (Translator's note)

23. On April 20, 1851, an attempted military coup sought to prevent Manuel Montt from taking power as president of the

Republic. Some civilians also took part, among them some of the "Girondins of Chile" and members of the dissolved Egalitarian Society. The coup failed, and Montt became president.

24. General Cruz was a Liberal (Pipiolo) candidate for president in 1851 who was defeated by Montt. He attempted to block Montt's victory, but his troops were defeated in the Battle of Loncomilla.

25. The banks of the Maule were the site of the Battle of Loncomilla.

26. We have been unable to discover whom Vicuña Mackenna considered the second Robespierre of Chile. He was probably a political enemy from the time when the author was writing this book.

27. November 7, 1850, was the date of the dissolution of the Egalitarian Society. See the introduction to this book.

28. This banishment resulted from the dissolution of the Egalitarian Society, of which these men had been leaders.

29. *The Last Supper of the Girondins,* a painting by Raymond Monvoisin (1790–1870), shows a scene that never took place but that is recounted by Lamartine in his *Histoire des Girondins* and that inspired Vicuña Mackenna. The canvas, 340 x 235 cm., hangs in the Palacio Cousiño in Santiago.

30. We are not absolutely sure of this date, but we do know that Monvoisin was working on this canvas while he lived on his estate at Marga-Marga, near Valparaíso, and that he came to that city from time to time because he had his studio there. The painting was bought from Monvoisin by Don Marcial Gómez in 1856 for 100 *onzas* in gold and subsequently sold for twice as much, along with *Aristodemus,* another great study by that painter, to Don Emeterio Goyenechea, the present owner of both, as well as of *The Fisherman. Robespierre, Ali Pasha, Heloise,* and *Blanche de Beaulieu* belong to his sister, Doña Isidora de Cousiño. At about the same time, Monvoisin painted his two other historical groups, *The Capture of Caupolicán,* which contains some masterful details along

with others that are completely absurd, and *The Deposition of O'Higgins*. The former is preserved in Santiago and the latter in Lima, where in 1860 we saw it carelessly rolled up in a warehouse. Fortunately, we were able to have this remarkable canvas photographed, and the photograph was reproduced in an engraving known as *The Ostracism of O'Higgins*. And those, as far as we know, are all the historical paintings by Monvoisin that exist in Chile. His *Elisa Bravo* was in Paris in 1870. (Author's note)

31. "La source éclairait des feux de son ardente imagination les gouffres de l'anarchie." *Histoire des Girondins*, p. 711. (Author's note)

Printed in the United States
By Bookmasters